Praise for *Expect Miracles*

"Mary Ellen has served up ... delicious, bite-sized morsels of inspiration that nourish your faith as they comfort your soul."

—Carolyn G. Miller, Ph.D., author of *Creating Miracles: Understanding the Experience of Divine Intervention*

"This charming book will awaken half-forgotten memories to the times when angels intervened and created a miracle for you. You believe it can happen again."

—Barbara Mark, co-author of *Angelspeake: How to Talk with Your Angels* and *The Angelspeake Book of Prayer and Healing*

"Mary Ellen is a truly gifted messenger, and her collection of Angel stories will uplift, heal, and inspire you. We are all surrounded by Angels, and *Expect Miracles* is one of their gifts to us."

—Doreen Virtue, Ph.D., author of *Angel Therapy*

"Mary Ellen is truly one of this planet's special angels. Her commitment to spreading the light is unrivaled."

—Arielle Ford, author of *Hot Chocolate for the Mystical Soul*

"Mary Ellen has artfully woven a joyous tapestry of modern-day miracles, as told by those who have been blessed with realizing the wondrous magical moments in their lives when they have been touched by the Divine. *Expect Miracles* affirms that

we all have miracles awaiting us . . . perhaps just around the
next corner!"

　　　—Judy Guggenheim, co-author of *Hello from Heaven!*

"In an age when the evening news fills people with worry and
fear, *Expect Miracles* is a welcome reminder that humanity is forever tied to the angelic realm and the forces of heaven. This an-
thology of letters and anecdotes is a marvelous daily reader of
good-will stories that remind us that life is rich with goodness."

　　　—G. W. Hardin, co-author of *The Messengers*

"Mary Ellen's book, *Expect Miracles,* leads us from the Valley of
Despair to the summit of the Mountain of Light. Each story
infuses the reader with hope and peace and reminds us all that
we are eternally safe in a benevolent universe. This book will
inspire and bring hope to many."

　　　—John Harricharan, author of *When You Can Walk on Water,*
　　　Take the Boat

"Mary Ellen's beautiful book, *Expect Miracles,* is like the iridescent
sparkling light that a rainbow shares. It uplifts you, touches
your heart, and brings you feelings of awe, childlike wonder,
and faith that God is all around us and that when we share
love with one another, miracles are too!"

　　　—Lori Jean Flory, co-author of *The Wisdom Teachings of*
　　　Archangel Michael

Expect Miracles

Inspiring Stories of the Miraculous in Everyday Life

MARY ELLEN

THE INTERNET'S ANGELSCRIBE AND
CREATOR OF THE *ANGELS AND MIRACLES GOOD-NEWS-LETTER*

CONARI PRESS
Berkeley, California

Conari Press books are distributed by Publishers Group West.

Cover illustration by Melissa Harris
Cover and book design by Claudia Smelser

Library of Congress Cataloging-in-Publication Data

Expect Miracles : inspiring stories of the miraculous in everyday
life / [compiled by] Mary Ellen.
        p.   cm.
    ISBN: 1-57324-158-x (pbk.)
    1. Angels. 2. Miracles. I. Mary Ellen
BL477.E86   1999
291.4'32—dc21   99–11459
                                                                      CIP

Printed in the United States of America on recycled paper

99 00 01 02 03 DATA 10 9 7 6 5 4 3 2 1

This book is dedicated to the Angels,
who make miracles happen in our everyday lives.

And to you, the Earth Angels,
who act upon their promptings
and bring the miracles into reality.

Never doubt that a small group of thoughtful, committed citizens can change the world; indeed, it's the only thing that ever has.

—*Margaret Mead*

Expect Miracles

Foreword

God created Angels. Millions of years later, God created the Internet (through the minds of some very forward-thinking geniuses). Then one day, God looked at His Internet creation and thought, "Hmmm, this Internet is a very interesting thing but I feel like it is missing a soul."

On that day God sent an Angel to put a little glimmer of thought in Mary Ellen's heart that probably went like this: "What if I created a newsletter with nothing but good news and put it on the Internet so that it would circle the globe and uplift the hearts of millions with hope and inspiration?"

And with that, *Angels and Miracles Good-News-Letter* was born.

Mary Ellen, or Angelscribe as she is known on the Web, is an Earth Angel who uses her computer to deliver daily doses of good news. Good news that is nourishing to the heart and soul. Good news that you can't find anywhere else!

Her newsletter is delivered on a near-daily basis and is filled with heart-warming, true stories of miracles, Angel sightings, inspirational messages, and so much more. Many folks say the stories renew their faith, give them hope, and inspire them to open their hearts. Such is the power of miracles.

Each day when I sign on to check my e-mail, I am always delighted to find a message from Angelscribe, knowing that for a few minutes I will be reminded that I am a spiritual being with a deep connection to the universe—something I find quite useful when I am in the midst of multitasking madness at my office!

I have never met Mary Ellen except via computer, but I feel like she is part of my family. Every day I receive her thoughtful messages, and we often have long electronic discussions. I am told that she is part Peter Pan, part Pollyanna and part Mary Poppins—a delightful combination that, in this case, isn't make-believe.

Expect Miracles is a very special book, especially for those who are not yet connected to the Internet. And for those online subscribers, it can never hurt to be reminded of the really important things like love, miracles, Angels, hope, and faith. Savor the stories in this book and then share them with a friend.

Arielle Ford
La Jolla, California

Opening to Love

*Miracles happen every day and people need to know
this . . . they can look for miracles in their lives. The
Good News is—there still is good news in our lives.*

—*Mary Ellen*

MIRACLES ALWAYS HAPPEN to me. I believe in them,
and am always excited when another one occurs.
Sometimes they can take a long time to happen. But, as
I say, it takes rain to make rainbows. I know, because I
was in an unhappy marriage. My husband was
immersed in his career, doing the work of five men.
There was no time for me, and I felt engulfed in loneliness. We had no communication, and we were even
sleeping in separate rooms.

Because I love to write and to inspire others, I took the emptiness in my marriage and created a way to fill my days. I began writing and sharing inspirational messages of Love and kindness. I shared these messages with friends, and later, when I became brave enough, I began sharing them with total strangers. They all *loved* them.

I knew Angels were guiding me. I could not see them, but I knew the Angels and I were a Divine team, working to inspire others. I believed that if I asked to be a vehicle for God's Love to work through me, then the Angels would guide me to wherever I needed to be.

When my mother gave me a computer in 1996, I began to share my inspirational messages on the Internet. It seemed natural to share my miracle stories and the messages with others online, to inspire them, to give them hope, and to teach them that they could expect miracles in their lives, too. And so the *Angels and Miracles Good-News-Letter* was born, to uplift hearts and bring Light to others' lives.

Oh, and what about my marriage? I must confess I thought it was beyond a miracle, but this is what happened:

One weekend, I went to an Angel retreat. We walked in the mud, ate tofu, and asked for angelic guidance. The facilitator, G. W. Hardin, co-author of *The Messengers*, asked Archangel Michael for guidance during the workshop.

I awoke the next morning with the phrase "Teach only Love" in my head. I thought, *How can I teach Love in my newsletter, if I don't live it in my own home?* I called Howard at work and said that I loved him and missed him. Howard started to cry, and said that he loved and missed me too.

We are now a couple again. Kind and gentle in his interactions with me, Howard's heart is totally opened. He admits that he was not connected to me for years. And he has no idea what caused the change.

When Howard was moving his things back into my room, he found his little white Church of England prayerbook, which he hadn't looked at in years. He casually picked it up and it opened to the page reading, "St. Michael and all the Angels: O everlasting God, who hast ordained and constituted the services of Angels and men in a wonderful order: Mercifully grant, that as thy holy Angels always do thee service in heaven, so by thy appointment they may succor and defend us on earth: through Jesus Christ our Lord: Amen."

I thought, *No way, not another miracle! And one by Archangel Michael!* I flipped through the rest of the prayerbook to find another quote, word, or mention of Michael, but all I found was the one page Howard had "accidentally" opened to.

It was obvious that the Angels had been at work. I carried the prayerbook downstairs to the computer, so that I could send the passage to my friends who had attended the Angel retreat. As I sent the e-mail, I wandered into the kitchen to get a drink of water. The time on the stove was 11:11. Angel Time.

Two days later, when our daughter, Ariel, bounced into the house after swim practice, she saw the prayerbook on the computer desk. She picked it up, and darned if she too didn't open it to that one page again! What are the odds? There are 244 onionskin pages in the prayerbook!

Ariel exclaimed, "Hey, Mum, look, Saint Michael!" I could not believe my ears. Only the eight of us who attended the retreat knew that the weekend was in honor of Michael and the Angels. Miracles seem to build on themselves until we are convinced that they are indeed miracles.

It is now much easier to "Teach only Love," for I feel that I was a humble student of its message. Now, with greater conviction, each morning upon awakening, I ask to be a "Divine Vehicle" in others' lives. The first few times I asked it, the most amazing things happened—somewhere, somehow, I was continually placed in just the right spot, on my daily path, to assist someone. And the practice continues to work. More times than are countable, people have said to me, "I just prayed for an answer to that question, and here you are telling me what I needed to hear, or offering me just the help I've been asking for." So many times that it is now common-place, folks have said to me, "You are an Angel, you showed up just after I prayed for some support."

It became obvious that something was happening—something wonderful. The more I asked to be a vehicle, the more I was able to help other people, and the more miraculous things happened to me. It *is* a great feeling to look for miracles—no, to expect miracles each and every day. My whole life changed.

I began teaching this simple technique—simply to ask when you first wake up to be made a Divine Vehicle. As others tried it, they experienced the same results. I've come to see that it is not about asking God/Spirit/All That Is for help or for guidance. It is about offering yourself in service to God, to Love, and then being brave enough to do whatever comes your way.

Have you ever helped someone? Inspired someone? And loved how it made you feel? Have you ever sat back and watched joy blossom on someone's face as they realized their heart had been touched? It is a great blessing of life to touch the heart of someone and uplift them. And this gift gives many of us the greatest joy.

It is as a result of the *Angels and Miracles Good-News-Letter* that this book has been created. The stories that are about to unfold off the pages and into your heart were all offered by newsletter readers from around the world, to be shared with people around the world.

Creating a newsletter was not my original intention. I did not realize the e-mails I shared so freely had become a newsletter until the readership had grown to about 1,000. Readers kept writing and asking to receive my newsletter, and I innocently was confused about what they meant. I was having so much fun writing and sharing my inspirational mailings that I was unaware of how profoundly they were affecting other people's lives.

By the beginning of 1998, I realized that a phenomenon was occurring. The mailing list continued to expand in readership, and it became evident that something was happening on a global level. People's desire for inspiration was like a dry sponge floating on the ocean of life. Folks from more than thirty countries wrote to say that friends from across the globe had forwarded the newsletters to them. I ran a poll and found that the average reader was sharing the newsletter with ten of their family members, coworkers, and friends.

Some readers said they had their own mailing lists of fifty, seventy-five, or even people to whom they would forward the newsletter. Many readers said they printed out the newsletters, posted them on bulletin boards at work, and mailed them to friends who did not have computers.

I am no mathematical genius, but it did not take long to see that the subscribers to the newsletter were only the tip of an iceberg of Love. They in turn created a readership that was growing exponentially. People asked if they could post the kindness, hope, inspiration, and Love that poured forth from the newsletters on their Web pages. This is how the newsletter, which was not planned, took root, grew, and blossomed.

As people read my true stories, they began to send me stories about their own miracles. They knew I would understand and would not ridicule their miraculous encounters; often this was the first time they had ever shared their stories with another person. They offered them in hope that the stories would inspire others in times of need.

The miracle stories were beautiful and moving. It was obvious that they needed to be shared as widely as possible, to inspire and uplift others, to offer hope, and to renew our faith in all that is Divine.

One day, a man e-mailed and asked if I was the person putting out the *Angels and Miracles Good-News-Letter.* He said he could not find my Web site. I e-mailed him back, saying I did not have a Web site because I had neither the time nor the expertise to create one. He replied that no one could create what I had on e-mail alone. My response to him was, "I expect miracles."

It is my deepest wish that, by reading these stories shared by people from around the world, you too will begin to expect miracles in your life. May you find a story in your life, possibly in this book, that opens your heart and mind and allows you to blossom into the great spiritual being that you are. It is my hope and desire that, as you read this book, you too shall open your heart and let Divine miracles flow through you to others, and feel your wings grow!

Teach only Love. . . . Expect Miracles.

Love and Light,
Mary Ellen Angelscribe

Breaking the Ice

On a cold snowy day, when I was about ten years old, my little dog Pudgy and I were taking a long walk. When we arrived at Ponca Lake, about two miles from my home in northern Oklahoma, Pudgy trotted out onto the ice and suddenly disappeared! When he surfaced, he desperately tried to climb out, but the ice kept breaking under his paws. When he saw me, his eyes locked on mine in a frantic, pleading cry for help.

I knew the ice was thin and that I might fall through, but I had to get my buddy out of that icy water. I lay down on the ice to distribute my weight, as my father had taught me to do, and cautiously inched my way toward him. As I moved toward Pudgy, ominous hairline cracks in the ice spread out all around me. I can still hear the eerie, crinkling, crackling, popping sounds they made. I was terribly frightened—I expected to fall through the ice any second—but my love for my dog was stronger than my fear. I pushed on in spite of the danger. My heart was beating like thunder in my ears.

Suddenly, I felt warm, soft, comforting hands on my sides and just above my knees. I felt light and ever so slightly lifted. I somehow knew I was safe and secure. My heart stopped pounding. Although I continued to creep forward, I also felt I was being moved slowly toward Pudgy. I began to enjoy the musical tinkling of the cracking ice. I was no longer concerned about falling through it. I had no fear!

I reached out, grabbed Pudgy by the leg, jerked him out of the water, and slung him spinning toward the shore. While still being gently supported by the hands, I backed out and then turned around and crawled slowly back to the bank. When I stepped off the ice, the soft-touch feeling disappeared, and I felt very heavy.

When I looked back at the area of the lake where Pudgy and I had been, little pieces of ice were floating in a very large hole. I took off my coat, dried Pudgy off with the outside of my coat and then wrapped him up inside it to help keep him warm and stop his shivering. When I arrived home, my mother gave me a big hug and was surprised to find that I wasn't the least bit cold even though I had walked all the way home without wearing my jacket.

When I told my mother the story of what happened, she said, "Your Guardian Angels came to your rescue; they do that when you have love in your heart."

Robert E. Parrish, Ph.D.

The Blue Monkey

Mother died when I was three years old. My sister, Suzie, who was sixteen years older than me, took care of me during Dad's absences. Dad was an opera singer, and traveled extensively. Eventually my father remarried, and Suzie moved to Kentucky, where all of our mother's relatives lived. After she moved I didn't see my beloved sister again for twenty years.

Growing up, I always had this feeling that I had "family" or an "Angel" watching over me. But it was just a feeling, nothing more! I grew up, married, and moved to California. In California, I discovered a church. I hadn't been one for going to church before, but something told me to go in, and I did.

The preacher and I became very friendly. One day, holding onto a crystal, she asked me to tell her about my life. When I had finished talking, she seemed to go into a trance and said to me, in a very far-off voice, "Look for a Blue Monkey."

I couldn't believe what I had just heard, so I just said,

"Pardon me?"

She repeated, "Look for a Blue Monkey." I left, convinced that she was "on something." Yet what she had said, and the way that she said it, seemed to strike an inner chord that rang with a sweet and true tone.

I went from shop to shop, over a very long period of time, looking for a Blue Monkey, to no avail. Finally, partly because of my busy life, partly because of the fruitlessness of my long search, partly because I did not really understand what I was supposed to do when I found this Blue Monkey, I stopped. I did not give up; I just stopped searching—or so I thought!

Years later, my sister Suzie tracked me down and the joy of hearing all about her life since we had been separated as kids was indescribable. Still, my inner voice kept telling me, "Don't stop looking for the Blue Monkey."

During a phone conversation, Suzie told me that one of our aunts, on what she thought was her deathbed, had made a confession. This aunt misjudged her time, however, and lived, and then was furious she had said anything. No matter, I thought. "Truth will out," I always say. "God has His ways!"

The confession was that our mother had had a child out of wedlock, something that just was not done, not in those days, not in the South. I decided to search for this missing child of my mother's. Once again I was on a search, not for the Blue Monkey, but for a missing sibling. My family tried to discourage me, as I had no name, no gender, no date of birth to go on. However, I had faith.

At one point, I hired a professional missing persons agency. They were unable to help, and said that having no information to go on, I would never find this relative. If the pros couldn't find this person, no one could. Ahh, but I had faith!

Eventually, a wonderful judge agreed to let me search the records in Kentucky. I did know that this child of my mother's was born there. Plowing through the records took me three years. By now I had been on a search of faith for almost twenty years.

Finally my labors bore fruit. I found my missing sibling, a sister named Mary, two days before her sixtieth birthday. Once we connected, we decided to get together for her birthday, the first birthday she could share with her birth family. As the three sisters—Suzie,

Mary, and I—gathered, we all could feel our mother smiling down on us, as if to say, "There, now everything is as it should be. My girls are together."

Mary looked just like our mother. She said she too had always had a feeling that someone was watching over her, and that she should be searching for something, but didn't know what! Not wanting to let her out of my sight again, I helped her move from Portland, Oregon, to be closer to us, her newfound family on the East Coast.

During the packing, I spotted something that took my breath away, and gave me the chills. Could it be? It was a Blue Monkey lamp. I had found my Blue Monkey!

Mary said that the lamp always meant something special to her, but she didn't know why. I told her my story, we hugged each other, and cried with joy.

Mary still has the Blue Monkey sitting on her dresser where she can see it when she first wakes up. She says that whenever she feels that life holds nothing for her, she only has to look at that Blue Monkey to know that God is right there, with her every minute of every day.

Bonnie Hartin

Is Faith Here?

It was the night before Christmas Eve, and I was alone with my three children (I have four now) in a tiny old wooden house in Southern California. It was very late, and the kids were all sleeping. I had just finished cleaning the house from top to bottom and felt like I'd accomplished a small miracle as I looked around me. It was probably the first time the house had looked so clean and organized and loved since we moved into it a few months earlier.

As I stood there admiring my creative touches, I heard a knock at the door. Forgetting that it was late at night, I eagerly opened the door to find a friendly looking young man asking me if Faith was here. He said he was just passing by and thought he would stop by to see if an old friend named Faith was still living here.

Well, I got the message long before he explained himself and quietly disappeared into the night. I didn't even hear a car start. What was he doing walking around in this quiet neighborhood in the middle of the night? I didn't know who he was, but I did know that he brought a message to me from my Angels. But I didn't know how to apply the message. I just affirmed to myself that Yes, I did have faith.

At that moment I had a very familiar body pain in my breast, warning me that I was getting a breast infection again. I was nursing my third child and was all too familiar with the early signs of what can become a very painful physical experience. What this had to do with faith I wasn't sure.

I knew that for me a breast infection is a sign that I am not allowing myself to be taken care of and nurtured. It is a manifestation of my anger turned inward about it. So this time I decided to give myself what I needed right away.

I packed my sleeping children in the mobile home I had borrowed from my in-laws and headed for their house fifteen minutes away. I knew I could rest and get tender loving care, and would also have help with the children.

My husband was living there temporarily, so it was a nice surprise for everyone. Though the children slept right through the travel, they would be happily surprised in the morning to wake up at Nanny and Papa's house, with Daddy too. Miraculously, all signs of an infection had disappeared by morning.

But the big surprise came early the next day with a phone call that woke us all up. It was a friend of mine who was trying to locate me. He was relieved to know I was at my in-laws. He said my house had burned to the ground in less than fifteen minutes very early that morning. The fire was so hot and fast that the neighbors on both sides had to jump out of windows to escape in time. The fire was still raging, and he didn't know we had left in the night. The firemen said that had we still been home there was no possible way we could have survived.

I lost my home, my car (it was parked at the curb too near the fire), all my possessions, and we had no insurance to cover any losses, but I had all my loved ones alive, safe, and happy. And the incredible love, concern, and gifts from people who didn't even know us but who read about the fire in the papers really surprised me.

So was that young man an Angel or just the messenger boy? And the message in the infection? Either way I got the messages that moved me to leave the house and take care of myself. Clearly our Angels were looking out for us.

I've been extra aware of Angel messages since then. I've learned to trust and act on them—now. For they always make perfect sense later.

M'IxChel

A Wonderful Visit

My husband passed away a year ago, leaving me with five young children. The grief at times has been unbearable. I have kept going for the sake of my little ones.

One drizzly Saturday afternoon, I was resting on my bed, not asleep, but very relaxed. I could hear the children in the background, the youngest ones coming in and out of the bedroom. Suddenly I noticed a bright and intense light. It was like the sun on the warmest sunny day imaginable, but it did not hurt my eyes.

From the center of this warm, white-golden Light, my husband came to me. It felt so natural. I could see he was at peace, not in the state in which he left this Earth. He was totally at peace. No more pain and sorrow.

It felt like God was allowing him to come to me with a message. We spoke through telepathy, not words; the message was that "my death was not a senseless act. It was for your best here in this life, for your life experiences . . . for your best." This knowledge penetrated every cell of my being. And as quickly as I felt this message, another one came through. It felt like unconditional Love.

He smiled . . . the most loving smile. The love he emanated was not a love that I had ever felt on this Earth—not a love conditioned on being someone's wife, or someone's mother, or someone's daughter . . . just pure unconditional *Love*.

I also felt this love with every cell of my body, and realized that at this moment, for the first time in certainly a year and maybe my whole life, I was totally and completely at peace. No anger. No sorrow. No grief. Just complete peace.

As I felt this all-encompassing peace, the Light grew brighter around my husband until it engulfed him, and he was gone.

Now I do not fear death or dying. For I know that there is nothing but unconditional Love and peace on the other side, waiting for us.

I also know that the greatest gift we can give to those who have passed on is to move on, to go on living—and live well.

Julie Elmore

Waiting to Go Home

A n elderly couple came to our animal shelter. They were very hesitant in their manner and spent a lot of time getting to the point of their visit.

"Maybe we had better go ahead and tell them that our daughter was in an accident and died and maybe they will understand," the wife said. They proceeded to say that their daughter had had a cat, but since her death, the cat refused to settle into their home without her there. They wanted to know if Mother Superior would take this huge orange tabby cat. They said they did not know how old it was and signed it in.

Our shelter has a no-kill policy. Unwanted cats and dogs either wait to be adopted out, or they live the rest of their lives in a kennel environment.

After the couple left, Mother Superior called down to the cat building and asked one of the Sisters to come and get the cat. Our Irish Sister Mary Brenda came up to carry the orange fur ball to his new home.

Usually, a new arrival is placed in a small cage or run

for twenty-four hours so it can adjust to its new environment and the free-roving pets. But, as Sister Brenda carried the newly abandoned cat into the room, it jumped out of her arms, leapt up onto a window ledge, and sat there, looking down the long driveway.

From that moment on, the cat stayed in that spot all the time. No one ever saw it leave its perch to go outside. Only Sister Mary Brenda, who had such a gentle way with all the cats, could go near it.

In the next six years we moved the shelter three times and took the cat, which Sister Mary Brenda nicknamed Kitty, with us each time. We always relocated the catteries near the entrance to the driveways. Once we moved the cats in, Kitty would take his usual place on the window ledge and would resume looking down the driveway. No one wanted to adopt Kitty, because he would not let anyone touch him.

Finally, we moved to a wonderful wooded property. During the day, the cats wandered outside onto fifty-six acres and came in to eat at night. But Kitty always stayed seated on the windowsill looking down the driveway.

One day, as Mother Superior looked out of the office window, a car pulled up the drive. After a while, she saw the car door open. Slowly, crutches emerged, one at a time, as the woman holding them carefully ventured out of the car taking great care with each movement. The woman moved slowly up the stairs to the office.

"I missed my cat over the years and have heard good news about your shelter," the woman said. "I've come to see if I can adopt a cat."

She had been in a car accident a few years before and had been in and out of the hospital all this time, with many surgeries, and now the doctors couldn't do anything more for her. She wanted a cat to replace the one she had loved so much before the accident. Her parents had told her her much-loved pet died while she was undergoing surgery.

The two women walked slowly toward the shelter. As Mother Superior opened the door, the woman with crutches started to step up. Suddenly Kitty jumped from his perch on the windowsill and pounced on the woman. She dropped her crutches and fell to the floor, lying on her back. The orange cat—the same cat she had loved so much before her accident—was on her chest. She hugged it for dear life as her cat loved her back for dear life. There was no doubt who the cat had been waiting for.

The woman never did adopt a new cat—she took her own beloved pet home with her. Now our windowsill was free for another cat.

Veronica Kelly

Miracle on Third Street

It was Saturday, May 3, and the third day of the Effortless Prosperity seminar at the deli on Third Street. Linda, the deli owner, arrived early in her usual white outfit, shimmering like an Angel in the sunlit morning. As we talked in the outside courtyard, she shared a secret. She patted her uniform pocket and whispered, "I'm going to give twenty dollars away to someone today." I smiled in return, because I knew she didn't have an extra twenty dollars to give away, but the spirit was in her voice, and in her soul. She was divinely inspired, and there would be no way to stop her.

There are homeless people in the area around the deli, and they often wander inside looking for a handout. The next needy person would receive more than just a drink or sandwich, he or she would receive a gift from the heart of this generous Angel. But, as it happened, the morning was busy, and no one appeared to receive the anticipated gift.

As the clock approached 1:30 P.M., we rushed upstairs to the meeting room to attend the next session of the seminar. We received our assignment for the day: Give some money away not because the recipient deserves it. Bless it. See how you feel.

"See," Linda expounded, "I knew even before the lesson that Spirit wants me to give this money away." "But you know," I said, "according to the lesson, it must be to an undeserving person." She nodded in understanding, but became even more vigilant in her enterprise. The busy day continued, and we both forgot our assignment.

As closing time approached, Linda informed me that she didn't have a ride home. It was late, and we were both tired, and I agreed to take her. Two blocks from her house, an idea suddenly popped into my head, and instead of going straight to her home, I made a left turn. "Where are you going?" she questioned in surprise. "I think we should drive by the hospital," I responded, not really sure why. "It's not far from here." She agreed only because I was driving and she didn't have much choice.

We approached the hospital, and I made a U-turn with the intent of taking her home. As we waited behind an ambulance, at the corner red light, Linda suddenly remembered the lesson and the burning twenty dollars in her pocket. "Wait," she said, "I'm going to jump out and give the ambulance driver twenty dollars!" "No, you're not!" I exclaimed, envisioning a twenty-car pile-up at the intersection. *But, Officer, I was only trying to give away this money!* rambled in my mind. I searched my brain for a better alternative and said, "I saw some people standing outside near the emergency entrance. I'll turn around and you can jump out and give the money to the first undeserving person you see." She was pacified for the moment, and I was relieved.

As I pulled up near the main entrance, there were three people standing on the sidewalk drinking Cokes and laughing. "There you go," I said. "Which one?" she replied. Since there were two women and one man, I responded, "A woman. The one with the glasses." "Which one?" she answered. I was dumbfounded. I only saw one woman with glasses. Linda carefully explained, "There is a woman sitting on the curb nearby with dark glasses." I hadn't seen her, and I was beginning to become frustrated with the situation. "Let me ask Spirit." I closed my eyes and thought for a moment, and the answer came. "The one sitting on the curb! Go on," I prompted, "do it!"

Without hesitation, Linda exited the truck, money clutched in her fist. I wondered about people's reactions: *Would everyone think we were crazy?* Maybe we were. Then I reassured myself. The motive was innocent, and in the true spirit of giving, I earnestly believed the Angels had guided us. But I still mumbled a silent prayer, hoping it was the right thing to do.

Linda approached the woman, bent down, and placed the twenty dollar bill in the woman's left hand. "I'm attending a class," she explained to the stranger, hoping this would not offend her, "and today the assignment was to give a gift to someone, and I am giving this gift to you." The woman grabbed Linda's hand and yelled, "There is a God!" My heart jumped. What had we done?

As Linda listened intently, the woman explained that she had been robbed and beaten by strangers, and they had taken all her money. She didn't have any money to purchase much-needed medication, and she was sitting on the curb wondering what to do. It was the worst day of her life, and she was praying for help. "I had lost all faith in God," she sobbed.

Linda stood for a brief moment to search her pockets for more money. There was another fifteen dollars in her other pocket, and she bent down once more to add whatever else she could. Softly stroking the woman's hair, she said, "You know that life is just a journey, and no matter what happens to us there is a lesson to be learned. I know that today was hard for you, but somewhere in there was a lesson, and you need to find it."

"I know what the lesson was," the woman replied. "I didn't think there were any good people in the world. I was wrong."

A taxi pulled up in front of the entrance, and the woman asked Linda to help her to her ride. When she stood, it was the first time that either of us had noticed that her right arm was broken and in a sling. As Linda opened the car door, the woman waved at me, and mouthed the words, "Thank you." I waved back.

We know nothing about this woman except her name. And we don't expect that we will ever see her again, but if we do, we want to thank her for teaching us both a lesson. She taught us how miracles happen just at the exact moment they are needed.

Sharon Mendenhall

Postal Marvel

L ast Friday, I mailed my miracle stories that would be
included in this book, and then went about my way.
Monday morning, the phone rang; it was the post office
in my town. They asked if I would please come in and
bring in some identification, as they had an important
document for me that was personal. I thought this was
quite odd, as I have an unlisted phone number.

I also thought, *Uh-oh, it must be another bill.* I've been
swamped with bills since my husband's death, and have
more than $60,000 in medical bills alone left from his ill-
ness. I thought I would go to the post office some time,
but not right away. All of a sudden I felt a warm tingly
feeling come over me. My Angel spoke to me and told
me to go right away, that it was good news.

At the post office I discovered that the envelope I had
sent the miracle stories in had become unglued and gotten separated from the stories. Ordinarily such papers
are thrown into the trash and forgotten. But the person
who was sorting the mail said he got a feeling he should

read them to see if they were important and if he could locate their owner. He read the miracle stories, saw my name and phone number, gave the documents to the postmaster, and together they called me.

Oh dear, I thought. *These stories were supposed to have been there by May 20.* I'm on a fixed income and only get paid once a month. I had spent my last 50 cents to mail the package on Friday. I thanked the postal workers and started to leave.

The men asked if I wanted to get another envelope and mail it again while I was there. I thanked them and explained about the May 20 deadline—the package would not get there on time now. They suggested priority mail, and I told them I couldn't afford it. Then they offered me the three dollars it would cost to send it.

I thanked them and asked if I could come in on June 1 and pay them for their kindness. They said No, just to see the story if it got published was miracle enough.

If only everyone would heed that still, quiet voice that speaks to them from inside their hearts, they too could discover the miracle of Angels.

Myrna L. Smith

A Timely Rescue

When I was fifteen, I lived on a farm in Wyoming. My father had abandoned the family, and my mother and siblings and I were trying to survive on the farm.

One day, a sudden hailstorm swept across the county, wiping out everything in its path. My mother saw the dark clouds and hail approaching. We couldn't afford to lose our crops! She said, "Boys, get down on your knees, and pray like you have never prayed before." So we all got down on our knees and prayed using my mother's great faith in her God. We watched the drama take place.

We will never know if it was because of my mother, or our prayers, or whether it was a freak of nature, but as we watched, the hailstorm moved toward us. When it reached our fence line, it stopped and never entered our acreage. The storm did much destruction and damage to our neighbor's property, but avoided us completely.

This happened more than sixty years ago, and it is still as clear a miracle as anything I have seen since.

Robert Stillwell, D.C.

It Started in Seattle

My mother-in-law was watching *20/20* one evening. The show was about Sister Emmanuel, a nun in Egypt who was dedicating her retirement years to the poor and homeless in Cairo. Knowing of my interest in Egypt—I own and manage an Egyptian import business and travel there often—my mother-in-law called and told me to tune in. When I saw the show, I knew I had to help. I ordered the transcript and set out to see what I could do.

I asked everyone who was coming to a baby shower at my home that week to bring a washcloth and soap. They thought I was nuts until I told them why. I called my dentist and doctor and asked what kind of medicines would be needed in poverty conditions and got those. I collected toothbrushes, bandages, clothing, and children's books until I had several bulging suitcases to take to Cairo with me.

I was going with a group on my next trip to Egypt, and I asked some of the group members to help. Eight other people were kind enough to bring pens, coloring books, clothes, and various toys.

On our arrival in Cairo, I suddenly realized I did not know what to do with the mountain of supplies we had brought. I had no idea how to find Sister Emmanuel in Cairo, a city of 44.7 million people that is growing at a rate of nearly 3 percent annually. Finding her would be like looking for a needle in a haystack, and I had no idea where to start.

I asked the hotel manager if he could help me find this healer of the poor. By afternoon, he had located her mission. But he had discovered she was out of the country and would not be back until I had returned to Seattle. He offered to store the goods and present them to the Sister for me.

But that is not the miracle. The miracle is how our intentions lead to miracles that go beyond our individual actions.

The hotel manager shared the story of my mission to help the mysterious Sister Emmanuel with other people who were staying at the hotel. Two of the people he talked with were a man and a woman who worked with the World Wide Health Care Project for the Poor. They had never heard of Sister Emmanuel and her work to help the poor. These people were staying in Cairo longer than I could, and they were there to meet her when Sister Emmanuel collected the goods. They were able to get her funding for a health care clinic for her garbage-city residents!

In addition, when the hotel manager saw Sister Emmanuel, he realized that she often came into the hotel to use the pay phone. Now, she has free phone privileges in his hotel.

It was three years before I was able to meet Sister Emmanuel in person. She speaks French and Arabic and very little English, but we were able to talk through the words of Love. The last time I was in Cairo, I discovered that they needed only fifty dollars more to vaccinate sixty-six children, and was honored to be able to give the money. Through this, I've learned that one person can make a difference—and it could be you.

Atira Hatton

Romeo's Guardian Angels

My cat is a fluffy Himalayan with huge blue eyes and cream-colored fur. He has the strongest personality of any animal I have ever known, and everyone who meets him falls in love with him. Hence, his name— Romeo. In fact, if you put your face close to Romeo, he will put his tiny mouth close to yours as if he's kissing you.

Most of the time, Romeo is well behaved. Sure, he bosses my husband and me around by insisting that his plate be constantly overflowing with fresh food, and it has to be the most expensive brand of cat food or he won't touch it. But beyond this idiosyncrasy, Romeo never gave us any trouble...until one day, when he climbed onto the roof of our two-story home. Since the roof is made of tile and sits at a steep angle, I was afraid that Romeo would slip and hurt himself. I know that cats are resilient in falls, but I also feared that Romeo— a lifelong declawed house cat—might run away from home following the terror of falling from the roof.

I ran to a window that adjoins the roof and pried open the screen, hoping to be able to reach Romeo. But he stood about two feet away from my outstretched arms. Too frightened to step out onto the slippery roof, I loudly pleaded with Romeo to come to me. He looked at me and blinked sleepily, but made no motion to walk in my direction.

I looked at my watch. My husband and I were scheduled to leave the house soon for an important meeting. How could we leave the house with Romeo stranded on the roof? Finally, I realized that I'd neglected to pray about the situation. In the past, my prayers had always resulted in speedy action from the universe. But so often, in the midst of crisis, I would forget to ask for spiritual help until I'd realize that my solo human efforts were ineffective.

It occurred to me to ask Romeo's Guardian Angels for help. Although I had never consciously thought about my cat having Angels, at that moment, it seemed like a perfect solution. After all, doesn't everyone have Guardian Angels? Why would animals be excluded from this gift from God?

I closed my eyes and directed my prayers to my cat's Guardian Angels: "Please, tell Romeo to come to me at the window and allow me to pick him up off of the roof." A wave of peacefulness washed over me as I opened my eyes. I felt compelled to say, "Romeo, come here," and this time, it worked!

Romeo walked over to me and allowed me to lift him into the house. My cat was safely in my arms as I shed tears of gratitude for the immediate help given by Romeo's Guardian Angels. I learned that day that everyone, including animals, is surrounded by Guardian Angels who provide Love and protection.

Doreen Virtue, Ph.D.

Photographic Memory

It was Sunday, February 23, 1997, and I was the passenger in a rental Pontiac Grand Am driven by my business partner, Jeffrey. It was mid-afternoon. Professional photographers, we were in Saguaro National Park to photograph some petroglyphs. We had spent the morning photographing the Colorado Rockies baseball team during spring training in Tucson, and decided that before we'd drive back to where we were staying in Phoenix, we'd take some photographs in Saguaro.

Jeff mentioned he was tired and could use a nap. After studying the map, I told him to turn at the next road, which was still a short ways ahead. I was also tired and was enjoying the car's air conditioning while looking out my side window.

Just as I was admiring a particularly magnificent cactus, I felt Jeff slow to make the left turn. The road slowly came into my field of view. Suddenly I shouted, "Jeff!" Coming at us only twenty feet away was an older car. The driver was looking right at me.

I heard the screeching of tires. Then, like we've all heard recounted many times, time slowed down. I watched this large, old car coming right at me. I remember thinking, *Please floor it, Jeff,* as I realized I was in big trouble.

The other car slammed into us going close to fifty miles per hour. We had our seat belts on and instantly the air bags shot out.

My eyes were closed. I heard nothing but metal crunching and felt our car spin around. I seemed frozen in my seat! We then hit another car that was making a turn onto the road we had been on. We rolled backward, then slid down a shallow ravine next to the road.

We slid forward for five feet or so and came to a stop. There was an eerie silence for a second. I opened my eyes and saw nothing but white. My first thought was, *Uh-oh!* I thought for an instant I was in a white light, that I'd "bought the farm."

Then I smelled sulfur from the air bags as they deflated. Jeff was frantically yelling, asking if I was all right. I thought for an instant and said I was fine.

I took a head-to-soles check on my body. Everything

worked and nothing hurt. When the air bag had gone off, it made me punch myself in the face with the fist that I had thrown up at the last instant. That knocked my sunglasses off and cut my nose and cheek, and some broken glass had cut my face in a few spots. But what I couldn't understand was why I wasn't thrown around. I would have expected to be slammed sideways into my door, but I never touched it. Nor did I get thrown in Jeff's direction to my left. The air bag and seat belt would have kept me from going forward, but not sideways.

Jeff jumped from the car and went to check on the others. Normally I would do the same, but I've never been hit by anything that hard before, and I couldn't move.

After awhile, I climbed out of the car on Jeff's side—my door was crushed—and walked to the back of the car and away a bit from the people and wrecked cars. I hadn't, and still haven't, ever seen an Angel, but in that moment I closed my eyes and for the first time ever, thanked my Angels for protecting me during that instant the cars collided.

The paramedics arrived and couldn't believe I wasn't killed or even injured. The park ranger told me I was one of the luckiest people he's ever seen.

Something inside me tells me that Jeff and I were saved that day, protected in some unseen way from being injured. I believe in miracles now, and I think a few of the others on the accident scene do too.

Kirk Schlea

Too Much Love to Leave

When our daughter Patricia was twenty-two months old, my husband's grandmother, who had raised him, passed away, and we decided to drive to Mississippi to pay our last respects.

On the way, Patricia got very sick. By the time we arrived at our destination, her condition was critical. Her fever was up to 106 degrees, which could have meant brain damage. We rushed her to the hospital, which was in a very small town. We found out that she had spinal meningitis, a potentially fatal illness that she developed from an ear infection. The medical staff tried their best, but they lacked the proper facilities and referred us to a hospital in a larger town. The doctor assigned to Patricia's case, Dr. Stockton, told us that if we had been another thirty minutes in getting there, she would have been dead.

My husband and I were very fightened. We had to alternate twelve-hour shifts in the isolation ward with her. On my shift, I was sitting there trying to figure out how I could fix her. All of a sudden, a strong sense of peace came over me. At first it scared me, but the longer I sat there, the more at peace I felt. This was the day of Grandmother Hill's funeral, and I just suddenly knew that our daughter was going to be all right.

You see, Grandmother Hill was a registered nurse until the day she died. And as I sat by my daughter's side, Grandma came and told me that the Angels were going to help Dr. Stockton and that I should put complete faith in him. I did, and within ten days we were able to take Patricia home.

At the time, the doctors told us that we would not know if there was any brain damage until Patricia started school. I am happy to report that she was in the National Honor Society in high school, and is now happily married with three beautiful children and a wonderful life.

I firmly believe that Grandmother Hill was the one who helped Dr. Stockton.

Donna Hill

A Double Blessing

I came out the front door as my oldest son yelled at me and pointed toward our old station wagon. My face went white as I saw the car, with my toddler twin boys in it, rolling down the steep hill that it was parked on. I ran like I had never run before!

From where the car was parked it was about 150 feet to a stop sign. Beyond the stop sign was a very busy road. On the other side of that road was an embankment going down steeply about four feet. Fifteen feet past the drop-off was a cinderblock building.

The car had already rolled halfway down the hill as I raced up to it. I tried to open the door, but couldn't. I had completely forgotten that the door handle didn't work from the outside. The window was wide open, but I never thought to jump in and hit the brake.

I frantically kept trying to open the door as the car sped down the hill, went through the stop sign, and across the usually busy road. Just before the car went over the embankment, I could no longer hold on. I stepped away in horror to watch the car go airborne so high that it vaulted over the cinderblock building and crashed into a car parked *behind* the building. It hit the other car, above its doors, with such force that it drove the wheel wells on the opposite side inches into the hard ground.

I was shaking as I got the door open and pulled my sons from the car. My wife and older children came running, all of them crying. We looked the twins over repeatedly. They didn't have a scratch!

A police officer arrived and kept asking, "Are you sure that they aren't hurt?"

And we kept checking—for days afterward. But they were perfectly fine! God blessed us! Our Angels were truly looking out for them, and us all! Later, we learned that a car coasting from the same spot where ours started could get up to a speed of 35 miles an hour before having to brake for the stop sign. How I was able to run even close to that I'll never know!

Rich Greffrath

If the Shoe Fits

I believe that a true miracle happens when we are given an opportunity to help another. One such blessing sits softly in my soul.

I live in downtown San Francisco, where homelessness is apparent in ever-escalating numbers. All the doorways are filled with vagrants, in every manner of disarray, and countless hands reach out in hope of a donation.

Tourists, shocked by the sight, are often generous, and our neighborhood is known as a good spot to "encourage alms." I, of course, am unable to give to everyone, and have set up a screening device so I can get through the day without being overwhelmed by the sadness and pain of it all.

One day as I was walking down our main thoroughfare, I overheard a youngish and semi-decently dressed man with no shoes telling an older homeless man that his shoes had been stolen as he slept. My heart ached. Imagine not only being homeless, but without shoes too, and in the city! My imagination refused even to consider the possibility.

I pretended to be looking into a store window as I eavesdropped some more. The veteran of the streets began to advise the younger, new-to-the-streets man on how to protect his belongings while he slept.

The older man walked on, and the younger one sat, head bowed, looking totally defeated and hopeless. I could not leave. I was riveted to the spot. I wanted to go and buy him some shoes, but I could not seem to make myself go over to him and ask his shoe size.

I walked a bit down the street to consider why it was so hard for me to offer something that my heart was straining to have me do. *What if I embarrass him?* I asked myself. *What if he feels I am intruding? What if I make it worse?*

Of course none of these thoughts made sense. They were my own fears—my mind trying to interfere with my heart's plans (as usual!). My all-too-many years as a New Yorker might have contributed to the hesitation, and perhaps some childhood conditioning entered in. Regardless of the cause, I was amazed at my inability to act.

A barefoot man. A desire to remedy that condition. It seemed to be a simple equation. Yet I could not make myself approach that desolate being. It was if an invisible shield was keeping me at a distance.

Finally, after much pacing and contemplating, my courage overcame my fear. I went over and asked him what had happened to his shoes. He brightened up, and seemed happy to share his pain and frustration with another. I guess it also felt good to know that someone cared about his plight.

I asked what size shoe he wore and what kind of shoes he would like. He lit up like a Christmas tree and exclaimed, "I've *always* wanted high top running shoes." Off I went to fulfill his wish.

More than shoes, hope was the gift. Since then, I have never forgotten during times of trial and challenge in my own life that at any moment help can come, often from the most unexpected places. That was his gift to me. Worth so much more than a pair of running shoes, wouldn't you say?

For me this was not a miracle—but put yourself in his shoes.

Marsha Stevens

Kelli's Miracle

My daughter Kelli had to have brain surgery to remove a large tumor that was growing rapidly. Courageously, she endured invasive surgery, chemotherapy, radiation, and gamma ray surgery. Her doctors told us she was the most positive minded patient they had ever had; she was fearless and fully expected to recover.

But after what appeared to be a complete recovery, she began experiencing a creeping paralysis of her right extremities and began to lose the ability to speak. After further surgery, a coma was induced to prevent swelling. Several days later, the doctors tried to wake her but to no avail.

During this life-threatening ordeal, a family member was always at her side, touching her, expressing love, support, and encouragement. The outlook was very bleak. Her chances for survival were slim. I couldn't imagine this vibrant, active young lady suffering paralysis for the rest of her life. All we could do was keep faith and expect something miraculous to happen.

She remained in a coma for six weeks and went into crisis several times. Five more surgeries were performed. How could she possibly recover after all this brain trauma? It would be a miracle if she even survived.

One day, fearing more bad news, I reluctantly telephoned her husband to see how she was doing. Steve said, "Kelli is awake and trying to talk. Would you like to speak with her?" Then I heard a very faint, sweet little breathy whisper, saying, "Hi, Dad, I love you." My spirits soared! My thoughts were, *Love triumphs again! Thank God! Love truly conquers all!*

Now for the real miracle. Recently, Kelli's doctors, who are usually cautious in such matters, said, "Kelli can go home now. After a few months of rehabilitation, we expect her to return to 100 percent normal functioning."

Robert E. Parrish, Ph.D.

Mrs. Brown and Her Nurse

Susan Roy, one of my student's mothers, is a home health care nurse. The week before Christmas, when she picked her child up from school, she had the most amazing experience.

Susan's office had given her a list of calls to make that morning. They sent her to attend to a new patient, a Mrs. Brown. The address was Apartment 111 at 444 Elm Street. It was Susan's first time to Mrs. Brown's apartment, and it was easy to find.

Elderly Mrs. Brown really needed Susan's medical assistance. Susan changed her catheter, bathed her, and cleaned up the apartment a little. They were having trouble finding Mrs. Brown's hearing aid, so Susan called her office for some help.

The office said, "Mrs. Brown does not wear a hearing aid."

And Susan said, "Yes she does. Margaret says she has had it for some time now."

The office said, "Margaret? You are supposed to be at

Mrs. Audrey Brown's." The office then asked, "Where are you?"

Susan said, "I am with Mrs. Margaret Brown in Apartment 111 at 444 Elm Street."

The office said, "No. You are supposed to be at Mrs. Audrey Brown's apartment. Her address is Apartment 111 at 444 Maple Street!"

Susan could not believe her ears. The apartment number, the street number, and the last names of the two women were identical. She finished up with her first Mrs. Brown then proceeded over to her second Mrs. Brown.

When Susan arrived at the second Mrs. Brown's apartment, the elderly woman did not need her services as much as the first woman had. The second woman had Alzheimer's disease and did not even remember that a nurse was supposed to come that day.

Susan felt that this was a Divine accident. She felt she had indeed shown up at the right Mrs. Brown's the first time, as her talents were needed and appreciated there the most.   ·

Kathe Kenny

Talk to the Angels

I had been tested lately in every aspect of my life. I was not satisfied with anything—my job, my home, my surroundings, not even my teenage daughter. I am hard-working, do my best to help others, and am usually a happy-go-lucky and optimistic person. So it's very discouraging when things get so rough.

Then I caught the flu and was in bed for three days. My bank account was exactly eighteen cents. I cashed in $2.30 worth of pennies so my daughter could have lunch money. Friends and family have encouraged me through bad times, so I called one of them, Margaret. She let me talk, and I cried and cried.

Then, in her wisdom, Margaret said, "You need to talk to your Angels and let them know that you cannot endure any more."

I got off of the phone and sat quietly . . . and told my Angels exactly that.

The next day, with barely a voice to answer the

phones, I went back to work. Then two miracles occurred.

The first miracle was that I was the correct caller to a Seattle radio station and I won $1,000! Then, about an hour later, my boss called me into his office and handed me an envelope. The envelope held a Christmas bonus—the equivalent of two weeks' pay.

First, when I won the $1,000, I thanked God and my Angels, over and over again . . . and cried. The second time, I realized no matter how down you are or how bad your life gets, you can ask your Angels for help— and they'll listen.

Carletta Leonard

Angels at Sea

M y sister Kathy is a purser on a cruise ship. One day, my mother called her to inform her about the death of my mother's sister Chris.

Kathy cried a bit on the phone, wishing she could attend the funeral with the family. But she was stuck in the middle of the ocean. My mother told her, "Aunt Chris is an Angel now—you can pray directly to her."

Later that day, Kathy was a bit teary. She was sitting at her desk when a man came up to her and handed her an Angel pin. Kathy looked at the pin and said, "You have no idea how much I need this right now."

He replied, "Oh, yes, I do." Then he walked away.

Apparently this passenger's hobby is making Angel pins. Kathy is still mystified why, at the exact moment she was thinking of her personal Angel, Aunt Chris, the man chose to come and present her with one.

Linda Watermeyer

Divine Vehicle

When I read Angel and miracle stories, I feel like my skin is too tight to hold in my spirit. After reading one the other day, I strongly desired to be part of a miracle for others. I decided to pray. I wanted to let God know I was open to being a Divine Vehicle for His or Her energy to work through me.

One hour later, there was a knock at my door, and my ninety-year-old neighbor Ruth collapsed in my arms. I called an ambulance, which my husband Dan followed to the Emergency Room, while I took care of the woman's ninety-three-year-old husband until her son returned my phone call, several hours later, and came by to help.

While Ruth was in the hospital, I realized how much I cared for her. Did you ever feel that you knew someone from another time or space? Well, I've always felt that way about Ruth. So I told her I loved her.

After Ruth came home, she knocked at my door, and there were tears on her cheeks as she hugged me.

The next day I found a note on my door telling me there was warm apple pie waiting for me across the hall—made from scratch! Every bite of that pie was steaming with her Love.

All in all, we spent about three days helping Ruth's family out. Dan has only one request: that I ask to be a Divine Vehicle less frequently than every day.

Judy Newman

Grandma's Help

My grandmother and I always had a unique relationship, unlike any I have had before or since. There was a special bond between us—we talked about everything and shared everything. She knew when things were wrong in my life without me even telling her.

When I was sixteen, I got pregnant, and she knew even before I did. She also knew that the baby would be a boy. Through all the confusion that went on between my mother and me about what to do, my grandmother stayed firm in her faith that God would prevail and my son and I would not be separated. She even began making little boy clothes and blankets and began telling me about my son—what a wonderful child he would be and then what a wonderful man he would become.

With her support, I did go ahead and have my son and keep him. The same thing took place four years later when I became pregnant with my daughter. The wonderful thing is, now that they are fifteen and ten, I see exactly what Grandma was talking about regarding my children.

Six years ago my grandmother passed away. Two days before she became ill, I wanted to cancel my vacation to Florida to go home to see her. But my husband and I were having severe marital problems and he refused to change our vacation.

I went with him, but the whole trip my mind was on my grandmother. On July 4, when everybody was having a grand time, I suddenly knew someone I loved had just died. I immediately called to check on my children, and they were fine. But the feeling of someone dying just wouldn't leave me.

When we returned to our house on July 5, I listened to my phone messages. With the very first message from my mother I knew my grandmother had died.

Two years later, after a divorce and custody battle, my two children were leaving to spend time with my ex-husband without supervision for the first time. I was having a hard time accepting this—I feared for their safety—but after two years of proving himself to the court, my ex-husband finally was granted unsupervised visitations.

The night before the children were to leave, I was up late praying for acceptance and protection for my children. Out of nowhere my cat started hissing at something down the hallway. I went to investigate and saw nothing. This happened twice more, once in my son's room and once in my daughter's room. The last time it happened in my room, and I decided to lie on the bed for a while. That is when my grandmother appeared to me.

The fragrance of her favorite cologne filled the room. The safe feeling that I always felt with her was there. In my heart she told me that she would be taking care of my children and that no great harm would come to them. She also reminded me that we all have to work through problems to make us stronger and that I could not completely protect my children from the world.

My children went to their father's for the summer and returned safe and sound. And I stayed at peace the whole time. For Christmas they left again, and again my grandmother came to me and reminded me to let God be in charge and she would protect them. Two days before they were scheduled to return, I received a phone call from my daughter saying that their father had disappeared. They were four hours away in Atlanta, and I had no clue how to get to them.

Finally a friend of their father's contacted them and then me. We met halfway, and the children accompanied me home. The children told me everything that took place. This experience did make them stronger and all of us closer. But last summer, when their father was granted visitations again, Tim, who was fifteen, refused to go. Stephanie, who was ten, had no choice.

This time Stephanie was more upset than I was. I let her know what took place before between my grand mother and myself. She asked me if she could talk to Great Grandma, and I told her to go ahead and try.

The morning that Steph was to leave, I found her in her room talking to someone. She told me that it was Great Grandma. I could smell her cologne again and felt at peace.

Stephanie had a wonderful time with her father over the summer and during Christmas vacation. She says that it is because Grandma lets her know that she will be OK no matter what happens.

Lydia Brown

The Mysterious Car

Remember the end of all *The Lone Ranger* TV shows from the 1950s? When our hero rides off into the sunset with Tonto, the guy he saved looks at his buddy or his girlfriend and says, "Who was that masked man?"

That's just how I felt on Sunday night, November 9, when I was on Highway 29 driving in my car alone back to Green Bay, Wisconsin, after a weekend with my daughter in Minneapolis.

The road is often dangerous because it is only two lanes. And this winter it was under construction and as a consequence was narrower and more frightening than usual. It was dark and starting to snow. As I began to drive through the construction area, I noticed that some of the orange-and-white pole markers between the lanes were knocked over. This unsettled my stomach, which was already in knots from all the coffee I had drunk so I could stay awake. On top of everything, I was really exhausted.

I had been on the road for three and a half hours, and still had almost two hours to go. Oncoming traffic from the Packers' game was picking up on this lonely stretch and would continue for at least another hour.

It seemed all the oncoming cars on the highway had their headlights aimed to glare right at me. Nobody was in my lane, either behind or ahead of me. The headlights made my headache worse and increased my eyestrain. My body begged me just to find a bed and go to sleep.

The oncoming cars came in waves, and although their headlights lit up the road, I had trouble staying on my side, especially when the flow ended and it was suddenly dark again. The snow and sleet were making a streaky mess on the windshield, and I couldn't see the white line on the right side of the road.

I started to worry about the people who were driving those cars in the oncoming lane—Green Bay Packer fans who probably had too much to drink were just as tired as I was. They weren't normal drivers at this moment, and neither was I. But we all needed to get home in one piece.

I was feeling increasingly more afraid. If there was anybody within fifty feet of my car they would have heard my prayer that night, because I shouted it as loud as I could, I suppose thinking that Angels don't hear you if you whisper: "GUARDIAN ANGELS, IF YOU ARE HERE, PLEASE HELP ME!"

There had been no crossroads for miles, and no car in any lane but mine. Just then, a safe distance ahead of me, I noticed a car driving on my side of the road. I had no idea where he came from, but his tail lights were bright enough to keep me focused on my lane. He was going as fast as I was, and although he was in front of me, when I slowed down, so did he, and when I sped up, so did he. I was no longer afraid at all. He stayed in that position for the hour it took to get through the construction zone and the dark highway and into the next city.

By that time, the snow had stopped, I was out of the construction area, the Packers' traffic had dwindled to almost nothing, and I felt more relaxed. I got my second wind and felt confident that I could make it the rest of the way alone. I tried to follow the car to see who was in

it and give him a thank-you wave, but he disappeared
into the city traffic.

I smiled and thanked God for the safe trip. Then I
thought about the Lone Ranger. Who was that masked
man?

Kathy Berken

The Right Number

I was channel-surfing on the television when I heard my daughter's phone ring in her room. For some reason I stopped, hit the TV mute button, and listened to the message. I heard a worried voice call out an unrecognizable name and then say, "Please call me."

I went up to my daughter's room and replayed the message. Apparently this lady had called about four other times asking her daughter to please call her. I hit *69 and the phone dialed the number that all the messages were coming from. I hoped that this would connect me to the worried lady.

It did and she told me that she had been trying to call her daughter since the day before. She was worried because her grandchildren were sick, and she couldn't reach her daughter to ask about them.

She had thought that her daughter was avoiding her because she didn't want her to know how sick they were. But she was dialing the wrong number! I was so glad to be able to help her by telling her that her daughter was not deliberately avoiding her. The woman was just dialing wrong.

She thanked me, and I thanked God for allowing me to hear the phone ring and encouraging me to stop and listen, because I usually don't listen in on my daughter's messages.

Helen Doyle

The Edible Miracle

Over the holidays, my mother and I were discussing the "traditional" things our family used to do when we were growing up. One of the things all three of us kids absolutely *loved* was my mother cooking custard on the stove. First there was the wonderful smell of anticipation, and then the sitting down to a warm, not-yet-set bowl of custard.

My mother is Scottish, and this custard was a very special one, from England, called Birds Eye Custard. After we kids had grown and my mother moved, the Birds Eye Custard "sit downs" ceased. My mother and I had not seen Birds Eye Custard on shelves anywhere for more than twenty-five years. We thought the company must be out of business by now.

As we reminisced, we both were very strong in our desire to find the custard again and have another "sit down." But, alas, we knew that the custard was nowhere to be found. We talked for a solid half-hour about how much we wanted that silly little custard, but because we were sure it didn't exist anymore, we didn't pursue it further.

Less than two weeks later, I received a holiday package from my sister, who lives 1,000 miles away. Since she is on a limited budget, she doesn't send huge gifts. She had sent a big jar of homemade hot chocolate mix and a wrapped package with a note saying "You will *not believe* what I found shopping the other day. I was in a specialty food store just looking around and found BIRDS EYE CUSTARD! I know this isn't much, but I hope you will enjoy it and remember how much we loved to sit at the table and eat it warm with Mom!"

Let me tell you, no big or expensive gift could replace the joy in my heart from that little gift. Nor could a big or expensive gift replace the tears and pleasure my mother and I shared with *me* cooking and serving her a warm bowl of Birds Eye Custard!

Coincidence? I don't think so.

Dierdre Baker

The Wisdom of Youth

My seven-year-old son and I were both ill. He had an ear infection, and I had bronchitis. As we were walking out of the pharmacy with his prescriptions, the only thing on our minds was getting home to bed. We greeted the Arizona sun with our arms around each other, determined to make it to our van without collapsing.

Just as we were about to enter the parking lot, a man approached us. He was big, at least six feet tall and easily 240 pounds. He nodded at us, and said, "Ma'am, do you have any money to help out an old vet?" His speech was slurred, and I could smell alcohol on him. I looked up into his face and felt a tug somewhere in my heart, but had no money to give.

His face was weathered as only the Arizona sun can do. His eyes were dark and puffy, and one seemed to wander. His long dark hair was blowing across his face, but he paid it no mind. He was a Native American and was wearing an armed services jacket. The jacket was so worn and faded that it was hard to tell what kind it was. The green seemed dirtier than it actually was when set against his golden brown skin.

I put my arm up to my forehead, shading my eyes, as I looked up at him. "I'm sorry," said. "I don't. I just spent all my money on medicine for my son." I put my arm back around my son.

The man started rambling. I could not understand everything he was saying, but he was speaking to my son like an old friend. Suddenly he said, "Let me show you something, young one" and pulled the collar of his shirt down, revealing a huge scar that ran most of the width of his chest, two inches wide at its thickest, and a quarter of an inch at its thinnest. I did not know how to react, and began to feel a little panicked.

His voice became clearer, "You ain't talking to just any Indian, son. We won the war." I did not know if I was getting used to the slur in his voice or if he was truly talking more clearly, but I caught every word of that sentence.

We edged our way toward our car. And while I was debating whether or not to stick around talking to this man, a car tried to pull into the space where we were standing. I did not see the car, but the vet did, and he pulled my son safely out of the way.

He laughed, "Be careful now." For a giant his arm moved with a gentle grace that hinted at a great tenderness. My panic subsided.

I thanked my son's rescuer and explained that we needed to be getting home. I could not quite read the expression in my son's eyes. He looked confused; part of him was in awe, the rest of him was not sure what to think.

The vet reached out a dirty hand to my son, "High-five?" My son smiled. Finally the vet was speaking a language he could understand. They high-fived, and before we left the man told me, "You're beautiful, you're an Angel, that's what you are. It isn't every day a fella's lucky enough to meet an Angel." I was suddenly embarrassed; I didn't feel like an Angel, I just wanted to get home.

At that moment, my son spoke his first words since we'd left the pharmacy. "You'll win this war too," he said, and saluted the man who had high-fived him moments before, making an effort to return the favor by speaking a language the vet would understand.

The man just stood there. I think we were both dumbfounded, and I noticed tears in his eyes. "You all have a nice day, and God bless you both," he said as he turned away.

Since then, I find myself hoping the vet will win whatever battle he faces, but mostly that after this war is over, he'll find himself at peace.

Jessica Hartig

Back Roads

I was driving down a back country road toward my island home and had taken my eyes off the road for a second to find something I dropped on the floor when the car hit a ditch.

I didn't realize the ditch was so deep. I kept trying to pull the car out of the ditch, but all I succeeded in doing was banging my car against the dirt wall of the ditch. I realized I had to stop as there was nothing else I could do.

There is very little traffic on that road. I got out of my car, and another car pulled alongside me as I shut the door. A woman driver and her teenage daughter asked if they could drop me off somewhere. I told them I'd like to go to Stanwood, the next town, so I could call a tow truck, the insurance company, and someone to drive me back home to the island.

The woman said she could drop me off at her husband's office. It was on the island! She said I could use his phone. I thanked her and said that would be great. The woman commented that she didn't have any idea why she took that country road that day, as she prefers the freeway. When we arrived at her husband's office, I saw that it was in a body shop.

Isn't it interesting that the one and only person who was on that road seconds after the accident just happened to be married to a man who owns a body shop on the island I live on? Guess who got the job of repairing my car, to the tune of more than $2,500? I thanked my Angels that day.

Sally Harrington

Miracle Manifestation

In January 1987, my husband was battling for his life in the surgical theater of a Singaporan hospital. Internally, he was bleeding profusely. I was forewarned by a doctor who emerged from the operating room that my husband's blood pressure was falling nonstop and it was unlikely that they would be able to save him.

This warning sent me into the deepest sadness of my life. The doctors could not help him. There was no one around for consolation. I was helpless, totally helpless. I refused to accept this desolated feeling. I had to help my husband! I didn't want to lose him. I must find a way!

Very desperate, I closed my eyes and prayed. Now, I've never prayed, but at that moment of heightened emotion and intense, sincere desire, my mind was suddenly very clear. I visualized the Goddess of Mercy with her magic wand. She was in a long, soft, flowing robe, wearing white headgear and a warm smile. I took her to my husband. I begged her to stop his blood pressure from falling, so that he would not leave this world just yet. I visualized the beautiful goddess flicking her magic wand upon him.

The doctor emerged a few minutes later to say that my husband's blood pressure had suddenly stopped falling, and he would live. What joy! How grateful I was toward the loving power that had helped us.

Tania Teh Tanyong

The Nun and the Novice

I was only fourteen when my father told me I had to get a job at the Burlington Catholic Hospital to help pay our family of twelve's bills. The year was 1941. My position at the hospital allowed me to go from job to job within the building. One day, I finished working in the diet kitchen, so I said to the Sister, "I am going to the main kitchen now to see if they need help peeling the vegetables."

I walked down several corridors, turned a corner, and saw an elderly Sister I had not seen before. I noticed she was having difficulty walking. She held her arms very painfully and had a severe tremble. I easily caught up to her in the empty corridor.

"Sister, may I help you to wherever you are going?"

The ancient Sister replied, "I am going up to the Convent."

I said, "I have permission to go there, and with your permission, may I walk with you?"

We started slowly down the hallway to the elevator

75

that went to the Convent. It was an old elevator, the kind where you had to open and close the doors by hand.

We rose to her floor, and as I was opening the door, she said, "I know who you are," and she called me by name. "All your life you have wanted to be a nun. You will become a Sister and will remain a religious person your entire life. You will ask for my name, "Veronica," and you will receive it—but not in the first two communities that you are in. You will try to get permanently into the second community and not succeed, then you will be accepted in the third. But you will have a lifetime of struggle."

I helped Sister Veronica step off the elevator, and turned to close the door of the elevator. When I turned back, there was no sign of her!

I hurried back to the main kitchen, described the elderly nun and asked who she was. None of the Sisters said they had ever seen anyone who met that description. I immediately ran to the diet kitchen to ask the Sister there if she knew Sister Veronica. She told me the same thing—there was no Sister of that description at the hospital.

It all came to pass as Sister Veronica said. I entered the first religious community, asked for the name of Sister Veronica and was refused. Shortly afterward, because of pain in my back from a childhood injury, I was forced to leave.

Several months later I had back surgery, and a year later applied to the second community. I once again asked for the name Sister Veronica and was refused a second time. A couple of months later, I was not feeling well, and collapsed. I was sent back to my own family and was not allowed to return to the community because of my back injuries.

After some time of healing, I went off to a third community. I was asked, "What name do you request?" This time I was smarter. I was given three choices, so I wrote down "Sister Veronica, Sister Veronica, Sister Veronica."

Before I left the room, Mother Superior turned to me and said, "I guess we must call you Sister Veronica"—and I still am Sister Veronica to this day.

Veronica Kelly

The Best Christmas Present

I don't usually tell people this story as many of them snicker or chuckle and then I get hurt feelings. But what I am about to tell you is the honest truth.

Christmas in our family of four was always a fun time. But Christmas 1996 was tough for us. My sons Shawn and Kevin, both in their twenties, and I were still in shock from the death of our beloved husband and father.

On Christmas Eve, Kevin had to work until 10:00 P.M. Since he had to go to work again at 6:00 A.M. on Christmas morning, Shawn and I decided that we would open one gift each after Kevin got home and before we went to bed. We then would open the rest of our presents after Kevin got off work Christmas afternoon.

It didn't work that way. We were all feeling a bit blue; we missed our loved one who had always loved Christmas so much; we ended up opening all of our gifts, and it was almost midnight by the time we got to bed.

I was sleeping in the recliner in the living room. Around 3:00 A.M., I was suddenly awakened from a very sound sleep. When I opened my eyes, there was a figure standing by the Christmas tree and looking at me. It took me a moment to realize that my husband was standing there.

I was more thrilled than frightened; this had never happened to me before. As I moved forward to speak to him, he shook his head, smiled at me, and put his finger over his lips in a motion for me not to speak. Then he sent the telepathic message into my heart that he was just fine and was happy, and at peace.

My husband was there only for a moment and never physically touched me. Yet I felt as though he had put his arms around me and given me a special hug, just like the two of us had shared during our marriage.

Suddenly he was gone, and I was left, once more, in the dark. I went back to sleep. The next day, I didn't mention this to either of my sons.

When Kevin came home from work on Christmas day, he came in while I was fixing dinner in the kitchen and said, "Mom, I have something I want to tell you but I don't want to upset you."

He then said, "Dad was here last night. He came into my room, and I woke up. He was standing there, watching me, and I felt like he was talking to me even though he didn't seem to be moving his mouth. He told me he was happy and that I should help you with the things you need."

Shawn was not home yet, so he knew nothing about Kevin's and my conversation. Later that night, after everything was quiet and we were all sitting in the living room relaxing, Shawn said, "I saw Dad last night. He came to my room about three o'clock this morning and he looked really good, Mom. He would not let me talk and he did not say anything but I felt like he was telling me that things were going to be better for us now."

Unbeknownst to each of us, we three had received a visit from our loved one as our best Christmas gift ever.

Myrna L. Smith

Gussie's Visit

I met Debra at the nursing facility where we worked. She had a one-hundred-year-old patient named Gussie who had just passed on. Prior to her passing, Gussie had repeatedly asked Debra to pray for her. Debra promised Gussie that she would be praying for her.

The day after Gussie died, the call light went on in her empty room. None of the other nurses wanted to go in, but Debra did. As she went into the room, Debra talked to Gussie's spirit and told her that she had prayed for her, as Gussie had asked her to, and she knew that Gussie was in a better place now, and she loved her.

Debra shut off the light, made sure it was properly connected to the wall, and left. The call light went on a second time. Again, none of the other staff wanted to go into the room, so Debra made a second trip. This time, she told Gussie that she would be missed and that everyone at the nursing facility loved her. She left the room, and the rest of the evening the call light did not go on again.

That night, when Debra got home, there was a shiny glistening item on her doorstep—a glass pendant of an Angel. No note, no card—just an Angel lying on her doorstep. Debra knew right away that it was Gussie's way of telling her she was OK.

Gail Mills

Dad, I Love You

It has never been easy for my father to show his true feelings. The words "I love you" are the hardest for him to say. Just three simple words—but such great power.

Since I have been reading and learning about miracles, I have added the words "Expect Miracles" to my day. About a week ago, I was thinking very strongly that I wanted my dad to tell me he loved me. Even though I know, in my heart, that Dad loves me very much, I still want to hear these words.

Last week, I was at his house, and Dad was resting in bed. I went into his room to say Hi.

To my surprise, he peeked out from under the covers and said, "I love you!"

Carol Goldberg

An Angel at the Door

A friend I have known for many years called me one day in great distress. A few months before, she had an accident in which a car ran over her foot. She has had a long painful recovery with surgery and physical therapy. That day, she was worrying about money. She had no job and was concerned about her mounting bills. She would need a wheelchair for a while yet and couldn't go back to work. "What should I do?" she asked.

I could see she needed her faith renewed, and was hoping to find the exact words she needed. "Now, dear friend," I said, "don't you believe that when you ask God for help that someone could just walk up to your door and hand you money?"

She laughed and said, "No, I don't believe that for myself! I believe it could happen to you, but not me!"

Wracking my brain for some elegant words to help her, all I could come up with was, "Oh no. Don't think like that."

Just then she interrupted, "Someone is at my door. . . wonder who it could be? I wasn't expecting anybody!" She said she would call me later and hung up.

A few minutes later, she called back. A lady she didn't know had just knocked on her door, handed her $300, and said that she was asked to deliver the money to her.

No one owed her money. It was an anonymous gift. The church group she belongs to knew her situation, and it could have come through them. But still she didn't know who gave her the money, and the lady at the door would not tell her.

A few days later, she got $100 unexpectedly from another source.

Where did the money come from? The Angels told me years ago when you make a request it is none of your business where it comes from or how it manifests!

Rikki Renshaw

The Best Sermon Ever

This happened to me thirty years ago, back home at my family's country church. I was sixteen years old and was asked to do the Easter service. My mother had gone to the Good Samaritan of Hope Church as a child, and when I was old enough to drive, I decided to try it out. (Of course, a pretty young lady I was interested in also attended the church.) I thought I might go into the ministry, and I've never been sure if the church was trying me out or allowing me to try them out.

As I dressed in my finest Jock Penne suit and my only pair of Sunday shoes, I practiced once again my three-minute sermon and the worship protocol that I'd been rehearsing all week long. I was very nervous.

I got to Good Samaritan, a little church back in the highlands, about thirty minutes from where I lived, before anyone else. This was back in the days of segregation, and our white congregation shared the church with several black families in the community. I pulled up just as the black families' sunrise service was wrapping up. I sat in my old '59 Chevy and listened to them sing some of the finest music I can ever remember hearing—spirited and joyful.

As the service broke up, I finally got up enough courage to go in. After a few minutes of sitting in the front row wondering why I had ever agreed to preach, I sensed someone watching me. I turned and looked. Standing in the doorway were several of the departing black church members. Just standing and looking at this white kid, all dressed up, shaking, on the front pew.

I walked over to them and extended my hand to Brother John, the preacher and song leader. But instead of reaching for my hand, he gave me a big old hug. I had never before been hugged like this bear of a man hugged me. There was so much love and warmth in his embrace!

I said, "Brother John, I need some help. I am scared to death." I explained I didn't have any idea why I had agreed to preach on an Easter Sunday, or any Sunday for that matter.

Brother John sat me down and comforted me the best he could. He recalled his first experiences and how scared he was. He gave me some pointers and then said something to the effect of "Now, son, don't you never mind. I will be sitting out there under that big old oak tree and when you get uptight or scared, you just look out that window and I will smile at you and you will be OK. Me and Jesus will take care of you today."

Now, I had heard him preach before and was always amazed. He could, and did, hold me spellbound many times. I said, "Brother John, you know I would much prefer you be inside with me on the front row helping me out."

He said, "That wouldn't be right. This is white folks' church time."

Remember, this was about 1966.

Church folks for my service began streaming in from the hills and hollers, and I got more and more scared. I was soaked in perspiration by the time the service started. I looked out the window and saw Brother John sitting on a stump looking in the window at me. It didn't help as much as I had wanted.

Finally, it came time for me to start. I stood up and the first words out of my mouth were something to the effect of, "I will be right back."

I walked down the aisle, out the back door, and over to the big old oak tree. I went right up to Brother John and invited him in as my guest. I told him I needed him really badly inside with me. This time when I extended my hand, he reached for it, and we walked through the back door together hand-in-hand.

You could have heard a pin drop in that little church. We had always shared the church, but the blacks had never come to our services, although I frequently—as did other white folks—went to their services. Brother John patted me on the back and went over and sat down on the front pew. There were lots of stern looks from around the church.

I went back to the pulpit. Before I could say anything, Brother James, a deacon of the church, got up from the back row, walked straight toward me, smiled, turned to Brother John, stuck out his hand and thanked him for coming. Then Brother James said, "Lelander, I think that was the best and shortest sermon anyone has ever given in this church. What say we have Brother John lead us in prayer?" I sighed a big sigh of relief and ended the first, and probably the best, sermon I ever gave.

Slowly but surely our church became integrated, and we went on to fix it up, install a new roof, windows, new pews, and even a P.A. system. As I recall, all the folks pitched in to do the work. Most of the time Brother John was leading the charge, hand-in-hand with Brother James.

Brother John died in 1971. Brother James is now retired. I still get just as scared when I have to speak in public as I did when I was sixteen years old. But then I recall the hug from Brother John and the smile from Brother James, and I feel much better.

Lelander

A Shove on the Back

The summer when I was eight years old was going to be great. My mom was taking my sister and me to a family reunion. Cousins and cousins everywhere! This year some of the younger aunts and uncles were going to take us to the creek to play in the water.

Finally the big day came. It was just beautiful. The sunlight bounced off the ripples that drifted down the river and dropped into a larger pool. It was a blistering hot July day, and the Ozark spring water was a welcome treat to us. We laughed and played, splashing each other with the clear, cold water. Ozark spring water is very cold and beautiful; you can see several feet down and not realize how deep the water really is.

We all had to wear tennis shoes into the creek because the rocks were covered with a thin layer of moss so slick you could fall into the water faster than you could blink your eyes. We were trying to catch little fish and crawdads with our hands and place them in a small bucket. The game was to see who could catch the biggest. Suddenly I spotted a really large crawdad.

Now, if you have ever caught a crawdad with your hands, you know that you have to sneak up from behind and grab it fast. I came up behind the crawdad and was about to grab it when I lost my footing.

I felt myself go down in the cold water. I grabbed frantically with my hands, but only water went through my fingers. All I could do was feel the moss touching my fingers as I continued to slip down into a deep hole of water. My lungs hurt from being under the water.

All of a sudden, someone shoved me on the back very hard . . . hard enough that I was able to get a footing on the top of a big rock. As my head emerged from the water, I took a big gasp of air and immediately turned around to see who had pushed me.

There was no one near enough to have touched me.

But I have an idea who saved me that day—I believe it was my Guardian Angel.

Linda Johnston

Help Is On the Way

Lately my life has been in a tailspin. I had been doing a lot of praying but I must say my faith was wavering.

One day, I was grocery shopping with my three-year-old son. When we came out of the store and loaded my car, I discovered it had a flat tire. My first question was "OK, God, what am I supposed to learn from this?"

I had never changed a tire, but figured that I was about to learn. Everything went smoothly until I tried to loosen the lug nuts. I couldn't budge them. As I struggled, a lot of people walked by, some shaking their heads like *What a bummer,* but no one stopped to help. So then I asked God, "Please send an Angel to help me."

A man, pushing a cart, walked by and said, "Could you use some help?"

Not only did this stranger loosen the lug nuts, he changed the tire for me—and he also restored my faith in asking for help from God. All he asked for in return was that I help out when I saw someone in need.

Gayle Sieg

Baby Steps

It was Christmastime and I had to pick up a package at the post office. I was grumbling at the thought of standing in a long line. I was carrying my six-month-old son, Savier, inside a front sling.

As we got out of my truck, I noticed nylon packing ropes all over the post office parking lot. Some of them were cut, but others were intact. I thought to myself, *Someone could trip on those nylon ropes.*

Out of sight, out of mind. I hurried into the post office to retrieve my package. On the way back to the truck, I was thinking about what might be inside the package when I suddenly became entangled in one of the intact nylon ropes. I was wearing my rain boots, with the extra wide tread, which entangled me very well. (Picture a rodeo, where the calf has its legs tied together and down it goes.)

To my horror, I went down, front first, and landed on my baby. It took him a few minutes to start crying. I scooped him up and examined his head. We had landed on hard concrete. I could feel my scraped knees stinging.

There was nothing wrong with Savior! I was in shock. I *saw* his head hit the pavement unprotected, but he didn't have even a scratch!

I stayed in shock for the rest of the day as I replayed the event. An infant's head is fragile. I truly felt that the Angels protected my son. He had been spared brain damage. The next morning it really hit me: There was no way he could *not* have hit his head. His Guardian Angels had been "on the job."

Maria Morales

Snow Angel

W hen our cat Kizmet died, I went to town to look for an Angel marker for her grave. The store had a wonderful granite marker with a cat on a log. I bought it and a store clerk carried it to my truck. When I got home, I dragged Kizmet's gravestone across the back yard, and in doing so put my back out. It even hurt to breathe.

That night it snowed. Boy, did it ever snow—at least thirty inches of the heavy stuff. After the storm subsided, I went outside to tackle the mess, with my little shovel. (Our snow blower, as had so many other folks', went *kaput* in all that snow.) As I was whittling away at the mountain of white, my back started hurting again, so I asked my Angels to send some HELP!

Within five minutes, the neighbor's son arrived with his pickup truck and plow, and he started plowing my driveway! He cleared it in a matter of minutes. It would have taken my husband and me hours, working in shifts, to fight our way through the snow. The young man would not accept payment. I asked him his name, and he said it was Rob. "Well," I said, "your name to me is Angel Rob! A few minutes before you came, I asked the Angels to send me some help. They sent me *you!*"

He laughed, and said he had been to church Sunday, and the minister had said you never know when an Angel is going to show up—but he never thought for a minute it would be him!

A while later, I heard the plow again, and looked out the window. Sure enough, there was Angel Rob, going from house to house, doing one driveway right after another in our circle! He sure earned his "wings!"

Aynnie McAvoy

Asking and Receiving

I was having difficulty getting the cash to flow into my business as quickly as it was flowing out. At the time, our rent was due, as was my son's school tuition. The tires on my car were nearly bald, and we had not purchased groceries in two weeks. This was hard on my male-provider ego. I was feeling more desperate than I ever had. But I knew that there was a principle in nature: Ask, and you shall receive.

So I went out into my back yard, to a large cedar tree, and spoke to God. I mentioned my need for money and said that I would appreciate a change in my current business. I mentioned that I wanted to do something different, because what I was doing—publishing books—was not working. I wanted my new job to be my joy, and I wanted it to be useful and serve others.

A part of me doubted I would get immediate money in this way. I told myself that it takes a week or two for things to come in; yet I knew that was a limitation in my thinking.

The next day, at the end of another long, anxious business day, I received a phone call. The man on the other end of the line said he had been referred to me. He asked me if I did desktop publishing. I told him I did and he wondered if he could have some advice. *Oh, great, I thought, just what I need, to give more free advice and get no income.* He seemed a rather strange fellow on the phone, and I almost said that I had to go, but just then he said, "I am a businessman and I have made a lot of money." So I hung on to see where the conversation would lead.

He asked me if I would help him design an advertisement. I thought, *Oh well, at least it would bring in a little money, $100 or so.* So I did the work. The next day, he told me he was testing me to see if we would be a good working fit, as he was looking for a publisher for his book. He then asked if I would like to help him with his book. I said I would if I liked it. We arranged to meet and I liked him immediately. I also liked his book. But I still wondered about payment. He said, "However you like. I can pay you once a week or all up front, whatever you want."

I said, "Up front would be nice, I am out of cash right now." So he wrote me a check for $1,750. That was two days after I had prayed for some immediate money and a job I would enjoy doing!

More important than the money though, was the realization that the principle, "Ask and you shall receive," really works. And be specific about what you ask, and be grateful for what you already have, for we live by grace, not by effort.

Scott Miners

Freeway Help

When my daughter Cindy and my two grand-daughters left Southaven, Mississippi, to drive the four hours to Jackson, a very strange thing happened. Thirty miles down the interstate, her car quit, right at an exit to a small town. They were left sitting there trying to figure out what to do when a man pulled up, stopped, and got out of his car to ask if they were having a problem.

Cindy told him her car had just quit running and that they were trying to get home to Jackson, which was about three and a half hours away. He looked under the hood and said, "Oh, I see the problem. Your alternator is about to fall out, it needs a bracket or a bolt to hold it." Then he fiddled with it, turned to her and said, "Hurry right home, it will get you there now."

She thanked him for his help and, as he turned to get back in his car, he said, "You are welcome, Cindy."

Now, she never told him her name and no one there called her by her name. She had only the two girls with her and they call her Mom. And there was nothing lying in the car that had her name on it. She was so shocked she wasn't able to ask him how he knew her name before he drove off.

But that's not all. They headed out on their way and her car ran beautifully all the way to Jackson, and then, guess what? It quit running and won't hit a lick now. I don't know about you, but I certainly believe that God sent an Angel to their aid.

Sue Covington

Everything Is Going to Be OK

I was all of twenty years old, madly in love, and out on my own for the first time. My boyfriend and I were living together. We both had good jobs and felt very confident about the move and our relationship. But only one short month after we moved in together, I lost my job.

My life slowly went downhill after that. I held a few temporary jobs, but could not find a decent full-time job. Out of desperation I took a part-time job doing comparison shopping for a local grocery store. Even though I could set my own hours, I hated the job.

The financial strain put our relationship in jeopardy. I hated getting out of bed in the morning. The person who had always prided herself on being self-confident and in control was slowly disappearing.

On this day, I was feeling especially down. I procrastinated all morning about getting up and going to work. Finally in the afternoon, I got up and decided to stop at a local fast food restaurant to get something to eat before work. As I stood in line, I was deep in thought about the course that my life had taken. I was feeling very helpless, depressed, and alone.

Right at that very moment, an elderly woman took my hand, put an object in it and closed it. She then looked deep into my eyes and said "Everything is going to be OK."

She walked away. I opened my hand and there was a little rock with "God loves you" written on it. I realized that woman in the restaurant was my Guardian Angel. I also realized that God believed in me, and I had to start believing in myself. My life since then has not been perfect, but it definitely has gone uphill since that day. For I learned that faith not only is a belief in God, but also in yourself. Whenever I feel a little down, I get that rock out and remember that everything will be all right as long as I have faith.

Are people Earth Angels or are Angels Earth people sometimes?

Jamie Risinger

Oops

My friend Victor and I were replacing a hot water heater in the kitchen of one of the apartments in a four-unit building that I own. As usual, our Guardian Angels were there, doing their best to shoo away one tenant, "Mr. Murphy," who always shows up whenever I touch plumbing. This is a given. I know it. I accept it. I cope.

As I turned off the gas, something just didn't feel right. Sure enough, the pipe below the shut-off valve was loose. "Let me see," said Victor, who has no faith in my judgment about plumbing. (With good reason, of course.) While he was "seeing," I picked up the wrench to tighten the coupling. Still holding the wrench, I listened to a short lecture on "looking before leaping" and then put down the wrench, agreeing that tightening the coupling would have been a bad idea, since the coupling was cracked.

Yes, I could see that now. And of course, I could go to the basement and turn off the gas from the meter, if I really wanted to be helpful, which of course I really did.

In the basement, I was a little alarmed when I saw the gas meter moving more than I thought it should have been, but it stopped, so I knew I'd shut it off tight.

"Yes, it's off tight!" I assured Victor. Just then another tenant, Nancy, whose apartment we were in, came back from shopping. At the same time Victor was about to remove the cracked coupling, Nancy went to the stove to light a cigarette. "It's shut off," I told her. She heard me, stopped, and began feeling around in her pocket for matches. Then for no reason, she reached out and turned the knob on the stove anyway. *And the flame lit up as usual!*

"Just some gas left over in the line," I opined. We all agreed and waited . . . and waited . . . and. . . .

"I *did* shut it off tight," I insisted, as Victor and I went down the stairs to recheck it. In front of the gas meters Victor asked, "Which apartment are we working in?"

"2-L."

"Then which apartment should the gas be turned off in?"

"Ah, I believe that would be 2-L."

"And would you mind telling the court what the sticker on this meter says?"

"OK, so it's 2-R. Picky! Picky! Picky! But see, I did turn it off good and tight, now didn't I?"

Back in the apartment, I asked Nancy what made her turn on the stove and she said she really didn't know. We both agreed it sure was a good thing she came in and turned on the stove just at the right time.

In no time at all Victor—Mr. Efficiency—had the new water heater installed, and I was "allowed" to go to the basement to turn the gas back on, *if* I thought I would "not get them mixed up."

Now we had to relight the pilot in Pauline's apartment (2-R), the one I shut off accidentally. She works all day, so I knew she wouldn't be home, but I have the key. I mentioned to Vic that it was just too much of a coincidence that Nancy had turned on the gas, and I don't care what he thinks, I *know* I have someone special who watches over me, and him too.

We've had this conversation before. He's saying, "Yeah, yeah, yeah, come on, let's go." The minute I opened the door to Pauline's apartment, we both smelled smoke, and I mean really strong! He headed for the back, and I hurried to the front. In the front of the apartment, everything was OK, and the smell was fainter.

So I ran to the back and Vic was standing in the kitchen. He had a strange look on his face and the smell of burning wood was powerful. But there was s no fire that I could see.

"Look at this, Honey," he said, holding up a charred wooden cutting board. I touched it and it was still warm, in fact, hot in the center. At first I didn't get it, but then he showed me what must have happened.

Much earlier, before she'd gone to work, Pauline had laid the cutting board on the stove, and at some point it had begun to smolder because it was over the pilot light. I looked at her two sweet dogs and I'm not sure how many cats, so contented and trusting, and suddenly it dawned on me—it must have been just in the nick of time that I "accidentally" turned off the gas to this apartment!

I've lived in that house for many years and I know which meter is which. So you tell me, how come on that one day and at just that time, I shut off the "wrong one"?

Ginger Talasco

Sisters' Sighting

My dad had a stroke when he was forty-nine years old and became blind and unable to speak. Because of the loving care my mom provided he survived until he was seventy-four years old. Mom was a very special person who was given a life full of lemons and made lemonade.

I was very close to my dad, even though he became ill when I was eleven. On the evening that Dad died, Mom called me and my sister, and we rushed to her home.

Later that evening, my sister returned home and I decided to spend the night with my mom, so that she wouldn't be alone. We were in her bed talking, reminiscing about Dad, both overcome with grief. It was 2:00 A.M. and Mom suggested that we try to sleep, as we had trying days ahead.

I no sooner laid my head on the pillow than I was pushed to a seated position by a force that I felt was God. I was directed to look at an area of the room, over the door, where I saw my dad, sitting on a cloud. He could speak again and told me that he was fine; he was no longer suffering, no longer blind. He said that my mom had taken very good care of him, that she was his soulmate and that he loved her very much. He wanted her to enjoy life now, as she had devoted so much time and energy to caring for him.

Gathered all around my dad were people I recognized who had died previously: a sister, grandmother, friends, uncles, grandfather. They were all there to greet him. After Dad's message, a peace came over me.

As it was being transmitted to me, I was relating to my mom all the details of this amazing experience. But she didn't make much of it; she felt that I was grief-stricken and talking crazy.

My sister arrived at the door at 6:30 A.M., looking as if she had seen a ghost. She told me that on the way over she'd seen Dad sitting on a cloud, with familiar faces all around him and repeated the message that he had given to me.

Mom ran down the steps, shocked to hear that we both had had the same experience. My sister and I used to playfully vie for my Dad's attention, as children often do. I felt I was his "favorite" and my sister felt the same way!

My sister and I hugged and laughed after realizing that we had shared something that may never happen again in our lifetime. Mom was a believer in the afterlife even before this experience, but now we all truly believe. We hugged each other and faced the sad days ahead, but instead of wearing black, we all wore white. We all felt at peace in knowing just how much Dad loved each one of us and how at last, he was truly healed.

Joy Howser

The Blizzard

There was a snowstorm, and a friend of mine called. She was frantic. Her car was stalled, and if she didn't get it started soon, within the next hour, she would not be able to pick up her son at day care.

I asked her if she could call a friend, and she said, "I did, you!" So, I packed myself up and began the hairy ride through the snow-blinded roads. I got onto the expressway—the fastest way there, about fifteen miles—and as I turned onto it I heard a voice clearly say, "Put your seat belt on!" (I was not in the habit of wearing a seat belt.)

I ignored what I heard; I thought it was my imagination (like we all think when God is *shouting* at us). Twenty seconds later, I heard it again. Now it was more adamant: "PUT YOUR SEAT BELT ON!" I ignored it again. The voice came again, even more insistent: "PUT YOUR SEAT BELT ON NOW!" Finally, I put it on.

I was following a woman at about forty miles an hour in the storm. She turned off to my left, but I felt that something was not right—she had not put on her turn signal. A feeling that God gives one, intuition or something, came over me. I slowed down to thirty miles an hour.

Once I got past the exit, out of the corner of my left eye, I noticed something moving—it was her car coming right at the side of my car. I think she figured I'd be out of her way by the time she got back on the main highway, but I wasn't. I knew, instinctively, that I would be hit. I said a quick prayer that no one would be hurt.

She slammed hard into my car, and I went spinning into the right lane, just as another car sped up out of my path. I spun around twice on the icy road and finally came to a stop. I looked around and again thought, *I hope no one is hurt.* (No one was.) Then and only then did I realize that I had my seat belt on. I am convinced that I was unharmed because the Angels told me to put my seat belt on.

And my friend? I finally got to her and found that she had called AAA for help. I asked her why she hadn't called them in the first place. "Oh," she said, "I thought calling you would be much easier."

Mary Beth Phillips

Nadia's Journey

A stray cat appeared at the door of my apartment one winter morning. She was covered with mud; her paws were cut and scratched. I took her in, bathed her, and tended to her wounds. A beautiful Persian cat, whom I named Nadia, emerged. I've learned a lot about Love from her.

My neighbors were unaware I had Nadia till the following spring. One day they saw her sitting on a windowsill and came over. They were shocked—she was their cat! They had left her with a neighbor when they moved over fifty miles to our apartment complex. A year to the day after they moved, Nadia had found her way to a location she had never been to, fifty miles down a highway. She had found the right complex, but the wrong door!

Grace Newman

Seeing Rainbows

Several years ago I was involved in a car accident that left me disabled; six months after that, my husband had a heart attack. By all accounts, both of us should have been dead, but we were still alive. Even though both of us survived, I really didn't know why. I didn't know that God was watching over us.

I fell into a very deep depression. One day during this time, it was really storming. I felt as if all the Angels were crying with me. I was in a dark night of the soul, overwhelmed, panicked, and depressed. With tears streaming down my face, I called out to God, "If you are really here, I want a rainbow."

I walked out onto my patio and up popped a rainbow. The unbelieving part of me thought, *Yeah, right, it is raining and it is normal for rainbows to appear when it's raining.* So I said, "God, if you are here and care about me, I want two rainbows."

At that moment, my husband came out to the patio and said, "Did you see the second rainbow?" Then he looked out and said, "No, you couldn't have, it's on the other side of the building." By now my first rainbow had disappeared.

As I told him what happened, when I got to the point where I said, "God, I want a rainbow," another one popped up. Then I told him that I asked God for a second one—and another one popped up beside my first one. We both sat down! Then to be sure that I completely believed that God had sent my rainbows, a third one appeared.

Someday I hope to have more answers than questions. But for now, all I need to know is that on rainy days, I look for the rainbows. Even if I can't see them, or God, I know they are out there.

Jo Farrell

Ownie's Gift

Sometimes a miracle is just a change in how we see the world. My son Ownie was born with microcephaly, cortical blindness, cerebral palsy, and serious allergies. He is fourteen years old now and like an eight-week-old infant. Before he was born, I had a dream about him, looking just about as he does now. He was wearing his brother's little red overalls, but he stood off from us as I played with his siblings. That day, I phoned my mother to tell her I thought something might be wrong with my expected son.

When Ownie was born, I was very aware of his differentness, although the doctors would not confirm my suspicions until he was about five months old. It made our challenges even greater to lack the knowledge we needed to help him. Upon the confirmation of his condition, we were sent to various medical institutions to do tests, and the day he was at the University of Washington Medical Center I will remember forever.

We were in the waiting room, just me with beautiful Ownie in my arms. As he slept, an older woman entered and took the seat next to ours. I noticed that she was perfectly groomed—right down to her manicured, bejeweled hands. She noticed my sleeping Angel and asked us why we were there.

I explained our situation, and her response startled me. She stated that kids like these should just be allowed to die. I let her speak her troubled, angry heart, which spilled forth the tale of how her daughter had had a baby with serious medical problems. The little girl had lived a few years, with the family's life completely revolving around her. Eventually she died, and the family was left emotionally and financially devastated. None of them would ever get over that, she told me.

I realized then that she was deeply wounded and that it was her grief that had brought forth her judgment of us. I felt profound sympathy for her, which I did my best to relate. Then I explained to this lovely woman more of Ownie's story—how he had fought to survive, and the joy and pleasure I felt at his life being part of mine. How, although his care was difficult, he had seemed to bring such good things into my life. He seemed such a part of God. I explained how, if I couldn't keep him always, at least I had the honor of having him now. By now we both had tears in our eyes. My last words to her were, "Whom, of the three of us, do you think is perfect in God's eyes? I know it is not me."

Her parting words were, "Thank you. I had not thought of that before." I think her healing began that day.

Ardith Fowler

Hope from the Other Side

Dad passed away ten years ago. One Father's Day, I went to his grave. I was very upset at the breakup of my marriage, and my whole life in general. For over an hour, I cried and screamed at his grave and asked him to help me. I questioned my father, as if he were alive, and told him I needed his strength and comfort.

I left the cemetery drained and returned the next day, calmer. As I was leaving, two blocks away I met my favorite cousin Lou. He asked where I was coming from and I told him, "From Dad's grave." We didn't discuss anything I had said at the grave, and Lou had no idea what was going on in my life, or how upset I was.

That evening Lou was at work and dozed off at his desk. My father came to him and said, "Tell her I love her and that I am always with her. But, please tell her I am dead and cannot physically be there, but I am with her always." He then answered all the questions that I had asked at the gravesite, things that no one heard!

When my cousin told me these things, I fell to my knees and thanked God. I also thanked Dad for his love and strength. Needless to say, I went back to the cemetery to thank him for watching over me.

Laina Hill

Studying Assistance

When I was a child, my father kept us traveling around quite a bit. I went to thirty-two schools! As a result, I didn't have time to make a lot of friends. To enter yet another new school and have everyone stare at me was so painful I became very shy.

So books became my friends. Then Angels started showing up in my books in the form of elongated crosses in sentences that were to be on tests the next day in class. At first I didn't know what was going on, but then I figured it out. After paying a lot of attention to the highlighted areas of my books, my grades started improving significantly. It made changing schools much easier!

I am now fifty-seven, and when I read a book of any substance my Angels still light the way for me.

Bobbie Feinholz

The Only Thing That Matters

This past weekend I had my first chemotherapy treatment for breast cancer (following three surgeries), and my six-year-old, Josh, got the flu. Josh's temperature soared to 104.7 degrees even with the Tylenol we were giving him. As my son was getting sick from the flu, so was I from the chemo. Josh asked if I was sick like him, and I told him mine was different. I asked Josh if he remembered the boo-boo Mommy went to the hospital to have taken out.

I then told him, "The doctors are giving Mommy medicine to make the rest of the boo-boo go away. This is also the medicine that will make Mommy's hair fall out."

Then out of the mouth of my babe came: "Mommy, it doesn't matter if your hair falls out. The only thing that matters is I LOVE YOU. . . ."

And as sick and worried as I was, I remembered: Love *is* the only thing that matters.

Lin Bartlett

Quite a Shock

W hen I was fifteen, I went down to the basement one day. A pipe had broken and there was one inch of standing water, so I thought I would clean up. Without remembering that I was barefooted and standing in the water, I started to wrap up some extension cords that were lying on top of the ironing board.

That is when I noticed there was a bare wire cord, but didn't realize that it was still plugged in. As I grabbed the cord, it wrapped itself around my arm, and I realized that I was being electrocuted! In my panic, I screamed for God and Jesus and that instant, the wire just fell off my arm and back onto the ironing board. I couldn't move. I was in shock.

At the hospital they found holes in my left and right index fingers. The doctor said that was where the electricity had entered and exited my body, which was why I was still alive.

On our return from the hospital, my father went to investigate. We had no fuse box and no circuit breakers had tripped off—the line was still alive! There was no logical reason why I should not have been fried beyond repair. At that point I knew that an Angel had somehow stopped the flow of the electricity when I had screamed.

Kim Lively

A Father's Love

When I was eighteen, my father, with whom I had not lived for some five years, came back to live with me in Washington, D.C. Within about six months, he passed away from a lung disease. In the following six months I lost several of my best friends to accidents, violence, and drugs. With no father and very few friends left, my life began to collapse around me.

I moved to South Carolina to be close to my mother. I arrived depressed and very lonely. After three weeks of searching for work and being unsuccessful, I fell into a very deep depression (I had been steadily employed since I was thirteen) and wished my life would end.

I went to sleep that night, wanting not to be, and as I slept I dreamed. It was a chaotic dream full of blurred people and images. I watched the scene sitting on a curb, as if it were a bad movie. And then walking out of the crowd, as clear and sharp as if I were awake, walked my father. He came and sat next to me and began to talk.

I was aware that I was dreaming, but the clarity of his

image was very unnerving. Dad spoke with me at some length, telling me not to worry and that these were the best days of my life. He reassured me that everything would be fine if I were true to myself and to others. Then he got up and walked back into the crowd.

I awoke instantly, and lay there for a while, knowing what I had experienced was not just my imagination. The next morning over breakfast I told my mother of my dream, fully expecting her to be at least startled. She smiled a knowing motherly smile and told me she was not surprised. The previous night before going to sleep, she had prayed for me and asked my father to help me, believing that he could see me and offer me words of wisdom.

Before then, I would never have thought to look to an Angel for such advice, nor would I have believed that I could be touched so deeply by something or someone right here on Earth. Now I see help every day, in everyone, and I will never forget. Today I manage a restaurant, am a musician, and am studying to be a teacher, all the while being true to myself and to others.

Matthew Dickerson

The Beautiful Angels

I believe in Angels and have for over forty-five years. When I was fifteen, my mother and grandmother had to make a trip to Great Falls, Montana, to help settle Grandmother's brother's estate. Shortly after arriving, my Grandmother started feeling pain in her stomach. After a couple of days Mother took her to the hospital.

The doctors said Grandmother's appendix had ruptured, peritonitis had set in, and her chances for survival were very poor. Scared to death, Mother sat in the hospital room with her mother. Suddenly, in the darkest hour of the night, although she appeared to be asleep, Grandmother said, "Oh the Angels! Oh the beautiful Angels." She seemed to be actually seeing Angels about her in the room.

From that minute she started healing, and we were blessed to have her around for another fifteen years.

Lou Ann Apostolopoulos

Unlikely Helpers

Several years ago, I was driving through Pelham Bay Park to meet someone at the end of the subway line in the North Bronx. It was November and it was cold. As I drove through the park, the car ahead of me hit an unexpected slick spot on a bend in the road, and went out of control. Seconds later, my car hit the same spot, and I started skidding.

Both cars were fishtailing all over the road. The cars actually circled around each other without colliding. I was able to steer my car off to the side of the road. When I left the pavement and went into the soft mud, my right front tire sank into the mud, and the car flipped onto its side. There I was in the Bronx, on a dark rainy night, with my two children in the car, in trouble. The good news was we were unhurt.

Then I heard someone pounding on the car door and trying to pry it open. I reached up and unlocked the door. I looked up to see a dark-skinned man with only two teeth, wearing dirty clothes, standing above me, holding the door open. The rescuer spoke with a heavy accent and asked if I was OK. I told him we were all unhurt as I handed my two children to him. I accepted his assistance to climb out of the door, which was now the top of the car, since the car was still on its side.

I looked around in shock, and I couldn't believe what I saw. I was surrounded by rough-looking, muscular men in dirty clothes. My car lay on its side on the edge of the road. Some of the men turned my car right-side up; the only damage was a flat tire. Someone had run up the road and was waving a flashlight to slow down the oncoming traffic. Someone else had pulled their car behind a large boulder where it would be protected from other skidding cars, and had taken my two children there into a warm vehicle.

The men moved my car to safety. They could not use my car jack because the mud was too soft to support the car. A man positioned his car so my rescuers could work in the headlights. Another came forward with a tripod jack that would hold my car while they changed the tire. They got my car started again, and brought my children back to me.

I tried to thank them, but the spokesman said, "Don't thank us, thank Him"—and pointed his finger toward Heaven. He insisted on following me to my exit in the Bronx to make sure that I met my friend safely. When he saw my friend walk over to the car, he tooted his horn, waved, and drove away. I never knew his name, or the names of anyone who helped me.

Until that night, I had always thought of Angels as fair-haired, light-skinned beings with wings. I now realize that Angels come with dirty clothes, missing teeth, heavy accents, big hearts, and old rusty cars.

Fran Churchill

Love Begets Love

One night on a business trip, I arrived late, so I decided to have dinner in the hotel. As I was finishing my meal, an older couple came in to dine. They were holding hands and had lovely smiles on their faces. The couple sat three tables from me. I was amazed at the love they showed for one another. It seemed to strike home all the more because this was shortly after the end of my twenty-year marriage, and I still had pain in my heart.

My waiter was also their waiter. As I paid my bill, I asked what their bill was; he informed me, and I gave him the forty dollars to pay their tab. He asked if I knew the couple, and I told him, "No, I just wanted to repay them for the love that they were showing to each other," and then I departed.

The next day, my business meeting ended two hours before the flight back to Houston, so I decided to eat again in the hotel dining room before my departure. After I had been seated, the waiter from the night before came up to my table. He said the strangest thing happened after I left. When the older couple went to pay for their meal, they were informed that another guest had paid for it and were given my message.

The couple were amazed. They looked around, and then asked for the bill of two young couples who were seated together, paid their bill and departed, saying "Love begets Love."

I smiled and said, "That's nice," and ordered my meal. About forty-five minutes later, I had finished eating and was getting ready to head out to the airport. My waiter was nowhere to be found. I waited and waited, and finally walked over to the hostess stand and explained that I needed to pay for my meal and hurry to the airport.

She smiled and explained that I would not have to pay. The waiter and she felt compelled to pay my bill, she said, because of the joy that was brought to the faces of the elderly couple and the amazement of the young couples from the night before.

When I told her that they didn't have to do that, she said with a smile, "Love begets Love."

I have been back in that hotel twice in the past year, and the staff there have told me that at least once a month they show their love to a customer by paying for their meal, and they feel blessed that they are able to do so.

Eddie de Roulet

Never Really Alone

I do not like to travel alone but once, due to circumstances, I had to go alone to a conference. Not only that, but I had to drive the company car into an area where I had never been. All of this made me extremely nervous, so to calm my nerves I prayed.

To make myself feel more comfortable, I decided I wanted to find out my own personal Angel's name. So I asked. No answer. I asked again, and again no answer. Then I explained to my Angel that I was hard of hearing and asked for a neon sign.

I started going through the alphabet. A = Ann; No. B = Barb, Bob, . . . no? I did this until I got to the letter L, and I said Lillian. *Lillian,* really?

I kept thinking *Lillian.* It was such an unusual name for me to come up with. *Lillian?* Me being me, and very doubting, I said, "OK, if your name is really Lillian, then have someone sit across from me at dinner tonight named Lillian."

At dinner that night someone asked if she might sit down with me, as she was alone at the conference. Her name? Yup, you guessed it.

Maureen Johnson

Grandpa Returns

When I was about seven years old, my grandfather died. At the time, I felt my whole life had been taken away from me. I couldn't understand what happened and why. I loved him so much and I spent all my spare time with him. Now, he was gone.

At the funeral, all I could do was look at my grandfather in the casket and cry hysterically. No one—not my mother, nor my father—could calm me down. I didn't want to believe he was dead and that I would never be seeing him again.

Then out of nowhere, an old man came up to my mom and said, "Let me have her." The next thing I knew, this old man was holding me in his arms, trying to explain to me the wonderful place my grandfather was now in. I felt comfortable in this man's arms and I calmed down. By his presence, he let me know that I would be OK without my grandfather and that my grandfather would always be watching over me.

The funny thing is, we lived in a very small town of

about 1,500, and no one had ever seen this man before that day and no one has seen him since. But I know it was my grandfather as a Guardian Angel!

Ursula J. Lovato

Rags to Riches

One day a local minister drove up to our animal shelter. As he got out of his car he said to Mother Superior, "I have a gift for you." He had two starved dogs. The mother was a golden Lab and the shaggy little black dog was her son. He said the animals were so starved they could hardly stand up. Then he got back in his car, leaned out the open window, and said, "By the way, the golden Lab is about to be a mother again, and the father is the little black dog." And he drove off.

Mother told the kennel man, Jerry, and me to keep the two dogs in the same room for company as they had been through so much together. We took them up to the kennels and put them in the room next to the kitchen. We put blankets on the floor so they could settle in and get warm, and gave them some warm water and oatmeal. Later we offered them a bit of warm milk and wine to soothe their stomachs. Then we left them so they could relax and feel comfortable.

The next morning, the two dogs looked better. It didn't take very long before the female dog showed us signs of pregnancy. Jerry and I agreed we would not separate the two dogs as they were so bonded.

One morning we entered the kennel room to find spots of blood on the floor. Over on the blanket we found what looked like clots of blood. In the four or five clots we found two little puppies, each smaller than a newborn mouse. We cleaned them up and wrapped them in rags soaked in warm brandy. We thought the puppies were dead, but after a short time we saw a touch of movement in each so we carried them to Jerry's room just off the kitchen. We fed them with a tiny dropper, put them in a cotton-lined matchbox, and put a lamp over them to keep them warm.

Throughout the night Jerry always kept his radio on to religious programs. He used to say to me in a teasing manner that since it was a Catholic shelter, he wanted all the dogs to have religion, so he left his radio on for them. I found out later that Jerry would carry the little matchbox and the lamp into the kennel room and lie on a blanket with the dogs, and sleep with the puppies in between. When he would wake, he would give each puppy a drop of water or warm milk. He never separated them, day or night.

It took a while, but eventually they began to grow. But they still did not have fur. Mother Superior occasionally would come and look at them and say, "Don't expect too much," but they surprised us and kept growing. Eventually the hairless pups began to play and yap. We named the female Tatters and the male Rags.

When they were about eight months old, we took them to the vet, who could not believe that they had survived. We asked him why the pups had no fur. He said the mother dog's starvation had affected them severely, but he expected the fur to grow eventually.

After a year and a half the pups put on fur in patches. The mother dog was adopted, as she was now in good health. But the father refused to go with anyone; he wanted to stay with the puppies. He was particularly attached to Tatters, the female pup, and indeed the two of them lived out their lives at the shelter.

When Rags was three years old, his fur was still coming in, and what little fur he had was beautiful. We transferred him to the male dog kennels. One day, a very poor-looking woman walked up the hill to the shelter. We walked over to her and she said, "I want to adopt a dog and I have seen the dog I want." It was Rags.

After she left, one of the other people who worked at the shelter told me who the woman was—the wealthiest woman in town. She lived in a mansion, and Rags went home to a life of luxury. She put him on her bed, on her satin sheets. Rags had the run of her place, and every summer he flew with her to Florida on her private plane.

Rags will always remain in my heart, not for his rags to riches story, but for the hope he gave all of us in the power of the spirit.

Veronica Kelly

Hospital Visitation

I had to go to the emergency room. I had torn something in my knee. I am now in a cast from my ankle to my hip—so much for partying. But the most amazing thing happened while I was in the waiting room.

The wait was long, and I was in a wheelchair in a great deal of pain when a really old woman appeared, put her hand on my shoulder, and asked me what had happened. Her hand was so warm. I felt the warmth go all the way through me. She then said, "I know, dear, it must hurt. But God can fix it."

As the old woman spoke, the pain disappeared. She then leaned over and kissed me on the forehead. I told her she was my Angel; she smiled and was gone.

The pain stayed away for a long time. When the doctor finally examined me, he said, "Why are you so calm? There is major damage done and it must be very painful."

I smiled and said, "Oh, it doesn't hurt now, and I know God can fix it!"

Jo Farrell

The Bond of Love

Whch I was young, I had a baby. Later, I married a man who was a drug addict and an alcoholic. Within three months I was pregnant again. Three and a half months after that, my husband committed suicide. I was left alone with a toddler and a baby on the way. But that was minor compared to my other problem. During our marriage, I had become hooked on drugs. The worst—crack cocaine.

Suddenly I had the biggest struggle on my hands— trying to clean up my life, get through a pregnancy, and then raise two children. I would cry and cry for my husband, angry tears, asking him why he did this to me.

Then, one night, he came to me in a dream. I was standing by his grave, crying, asking why he had left me alone with this struggle. Then, out of the mist, he walked toward me. I started shaking. He said, "Baby, I'm not dead. Can't you see that?"

I asked him how this was possible. I had identified his

body. I saw him dead—so his being here wasn't possible! He said that he was, indeed, with God in Heaven; while he wasn't physically alive here on Earth, he was alive in Heaven, and was watching over me, my toddler, and our unborn son. (This was a revelation, as it was too early to tell the sex of our baby.) He came over to me, put his arms around me, and told me not to worry anymore, that things would be OK, our son would be OK, and he would always be there, watching over us.

I woke up feeling relieved. Never, at any time, since his death, had I felt such peace. Several months later, I gave birth to Matthew, a healthy baby boy. His name means "Gift of God," and he truly is. I'm living on my own and support my young children without help or state assistance. I work part-time and go to school full-time studying elementary education. I have finally reached a point in my life where I'm happy.

I have had several "visits" from my husband since then. He comes to me when I am extremely despondent. I always feel much better afterward. He came to me again last week. He told me what a great job I was doing with the kids and he was so proud of me for going back to school. Then he kissed me goodnight.

The bond of Love is never broken.

Nicole Burnham

Help from Above

My husband and I are on speaking terms with our Angels. We live thirty minutes away from Lake Worth Beach in Florida. We love to sit in our car and watch the scenery at the beach. However, the parking meters are limited. If you don't get to the beach by 9:00 A.M., it is virtually impossible to find an empty meter. But not for us.

As we drive over the Intracoastal Waterway bridge we start asking our Parking Angels for a perfect parking spot. Nine times out of ten, somebody will back out just as we arrive. A few times our Angels even found us parking spaces with time on the meters. It costs twenty five cents for fifteen minutes. One day we were given nine hours on the meter! Our Parking Angels really gave us a bonus that day!

At the local mall we like to eat lunch at the food court. Again we have a talk with our Parking Angels, who invariably find us a spot within easy walking distance of the front entrance of the mall—right near the food court.

I call on my Shopping Angels too. This December, I was out shopping for my husband's gifts and was wondering where to find a special CD. I was heading for a certain shopping mall when I "heard," "Go to Jeannie's Secrets!" I shook my head and thought, *OK, why not?* The next light was her store, so I wheeled into the parking lot and walked into the store. There was the CD I was seeking, and more music by the same composer, plus the Angel stickers I'd been looking for. I also found a special calendar I wanted to buy him. Thanks to the voices of my Shopping Angels, I was more than halfway through my Christmas shopping.

Next, I went into a store that sold the T-shirt my husband wanted. There were piles of them, but at a higher price than I really wanted to pay. I stood there and asked what to do. I "heard," *Stay here because you'd spend more money in gas and energy if you go searching for the less expensive shirts.* I picked up a shirt and stood in line. When it was my turn, the saleswoman pulled out a flyer filled with coupons and gave me two discounts. These discounts put the T-shirt three dollars lower than the sale price! So again I said, "Thank you, Shopping Angels, for all your loving help and guidance."

Jean Maurie Puhlman

Running on Empty

In the autumn of 1995, on the same day the Pope came to America, I had to drive my oldest son on a 400-mile trip from Long Island to Plattsburgh to visit a college open house. It was pouring rain, and somewhere in Westchester County, while on the thruway, the gas tank was registering empty. I had to get off the thruway to look for a gas station.

I got lost driving on a lonely road in the woods, and my gas tank was now past the empty mark. My heart was pounding and I felt panicked. I came to a stop sign, and out of nowhere came a red pickup truck with two men in it. I waved to them and asked them where the nearest gas station was. The two men smiled at me and told me where to find it. They said it was five miles away.

I told them there was no way I could make it to the station. They both smiled and said, "Don't worry, you'll make it there. You won't run out of gas." Then they drove on. I followed their directions for five miles, and sure enough, we made it to the gas station on a completely empty tank. I think those two men were Angels—how else could they be so sure that I wouldn't run out of gas?

Mary Ellen Szwejkowski

The Rosary Beads

A few years ago, I went to a place in Georgia where the Virgin Mary speaks to a woman on the thirteenth of the month. This particular month the thirteenth fell on Good Friday, and while we were saying the rosary, I experienced a miracle.

While holding the rosary beads in my hand, I suddenly felt some energy going through my body and also through the beads. Not wanting to make a scene, I peeked at the beads and to my astonishment, the silver beads had changed to golden ones. Afterward I shared the experience with the people near me and when I got home, with my husband. Unfortunately, he is very skeptical of these things and said to me, "It must have turned from the acid on your skin."

I was not convinced of that and went upstairs. Gazing in the mirror at the necklace I was wearing, I was shocked to see that the chain and the badly tarnished cameo shone like new. It was my grandmother's very old cameo necklace, which had filigree of gold around it. I wear it even though it has been blackened and the chain is too.

I ran down the steps to show my husband the necklace. I told him that it couldn't have been something on my skin, as my necklace was on top of my sweater. Not only that, but the matching earrings were in my pocket, because I wasn't wearing them, and they had been polished also.

Months later, my aunt was diagnosed with cancer. She is a very religious woman, so I sent her the golden rosary beads to pray with. She is now in remission, and I don't know that the beads were responsible, but I know that they were a comfort to her.

It sure does make you wonder, though.

Joanne Miller

At the Wheel

While I was living in Rialto, California, a neighbor's mother came to visit from New York and brought her four-year-old granddaughter. The young girl played with my three-year-old son and eighteen-month-old daughter.

One day we decided to pack a picnic and take all the children to Lake Arrowhead, where the elevation is over 6,000 feet at the picnic site. Everyone had a marvelous time, and the children played until they were falling asleep on their feet. We loaded up the baskets and kids and headed back down the mountain, with me in the driver's seat.

As the children napped peacefully in the back, suddenly the station wagon began picking up speed. I tried the brakes, but the car would not slow down. Faster and faster we went around those winding, sharp curves. The speedometer was going higher and higher. I looked over to the side of the road and could see how far down the treacherous mountain we would soon be going if I couldn't get control of the car.

I thought of the young lives in the back of the car. I prayed that they would be spared, that we would all be spared. I don't ever remember, in my life, such an over-all feeling of terror and helplessness. I rode the brakes, but we still continued to gain speed. "Dear God, please send someone to help me," I prayed.

Almost immediately I felt someone, something, take control of the steering wheel. My panic lessened, then I became calm. The car was now doing almost 100 miles an hour around those horrible curves, but it was being expertly driven.

We finally made it down to about the 2,000-feet level, and all of a sudden, I was given back control of the wheel and drove on home. My woman passenger, who had remained calm down the mountain, decided she needed a good stiff drink. I joined her. Many of you are too young to remember cars that had overdrive and regular drive. I learned after the fact that I should have taken the car out of overdrive before driving down the mountain.

When we told her family and my husband about our frightening experience, I was at a loss for words to describe that someone else had driven the car for me. When I learned of Guardian Angels, I knew who had been responsible for saving all our lives.

Margaret S. Taylor

Disappearing Roof

In the summer of 1976, my wife and I moved into a new second-floor apartment. One night my wife was at work and I was "watching" our two-year-old son. Regrettably, I was watching more TV than son. Suddenly I noticed how quiet it had gotten. I called out to him—and got no answer. I got up and searched the five-room apartment. My son was nowhere to be seen.

At this point, I was getting frantic. As I passed the front window, my peripheral vision caught a reflection of something outside the window. It was my son out on the flat front porch roof. In the dark, the ceiling light had bounced off his forehead, catching my attention.

It was dark. There was an old-fashioned streetlight on the road that caused a dull shine and cast eerie shadows, barely illuminating much beyond the road. I went to the open window, looked out at the shadowy figure sitting on the roof about five feet away, and collected myself. I knew not to panic and start yelling, which could startle him and cause him to lose his balance. So, in a calm voice, I said, "Son, come here. I want to see you." He crawled over to the window. I grabbed him and breathed a sigh of relief. Once inside, I scolded and hugged him, closed the screen and told him to never go out there again.

The next day, when I got home from work, I was still thinking about the incident and the memory of him on that roof. I walked to the window, thanking God for my good fortune the previous night. I looked out to the spot where he had been to relive the traumatic sight etched in my mind. I looked out and saw . . . *no roof!*

In the daylight, there was no roof at the distance I had seen him the previous night, which I guessed to be about five feet out. Even reducing that to four feet for judgment error, he would have still been in the air. The roof was a slim one, only going out about three feet and then dropping off steeply with shingles at about a forty-five-degree angle. If he had been only three feet out (and I don't think he was that close), he would have been right on the very edge or down onto those shingles. But when he crawled over to me, he crawled straight over and not up and then over. All I can figure is that he had some type of Guardian Angel helping him that night, and I thank God for whoever that was!

John Fitch

The Fireman's Lifeline

I'm a fireman. In the middle of August, on a very hot Wednesday night, I happened to stop by the firehouse on my way home from doing errands. While at the station, the fire alarms sounded, and we were dispatched to an apartment fire.

Upon arriving at the scene, we encountered fire and heavy smoke in the second-floor apartments, to which we extended an attack line. At the time, we did not know the fire was also on the third floor. And there was now heavy fire on both the second and the third floors.

We started knocking the fire down and thought we had made some progress. Two of the crew members with me on the attack line had exhausted their breathing air, and needed to leave the building to change their bottles before they could continue. I stayed in the apartment and kept the water flowing, waiting for two more firefighters to come up and back me on the line.

Before they could join me, a strange feeling came over me that I had never had before. It was telling me that it was time to exit the building and exit *right now!* The feeling was so strong that I dropped the attack line and made my way out.

No sooner had I gotten outside than the third floor collapsed onto the second floor, right where I had been! Had I not exited the building right then, I would have been crushed by the falling floor and burned to death before anyone could have rescued me from the burning debris.

From this and other miraculous rescues, I've learned to expect miracles and teach others to expect them as well.

Carl Dixon

A Winter Rescue

I heard this story myself from my grandmother and have no doubt whatsoever about its truth. A prayer cannot be said too often nor an Angel story retold too much. These events happened on a cold winter's night a long time ago, during the last decade of the nineteenth century, when my grandmother was just a child. In Quebec, Canada, which was then mostly farmland country with narrow and primitive roads, travel was by horse and sleigh.

It was Christmastime. My grandmother's family, returning from their annual visit to relatives, had already traveled many hours and many miles. Everywhere the snow glistened under the full moon, a carpet of tiny flickering lights that teased the dancing stars overhead. In the sleigh, the young family was snugly bundled underneath a buffalo blanket, and the gentle moon created a dreamscape that lulled the children into reveries about their happy holiday. It was cold and silent, and the family could hear the rhythmic crunching sound of the horse and sleigh moving on the snow. The hypnotic sound of the tiny sleighbells enhanced their enchantment.

Suddenly, and without warning, a gust of wind came up, then snow began falling fast. Soon the blizzard obliterated the small road, and the horse labored to keep walking. The snow was blinding. The travelers were lost, their sense of direction gone.

Thoughts of wolves, which traveled in packs and were numerous in those days, intimidated the group. Miles from home and in the middle of the cold night, they feared the worst.

As my grandmother's father got out to calm the horse and try to extricate it from the deepening snow, he perceived someone walking along the side of the road, head bent to brace himself against the wind. My great-grandfather thought it was strange that he had not noticed this person before.

The stranger approached and asked if he could help. His presence seemed to calm the horse. Just as the storm had come up out of nowhere, it began to abate the same way, and in a short time the blizzard was over.

My family invited the stranger to ride in the sleigh, and they continued on their journey.

As they approached the first village, the stranger asked to be let off. They stopped and he jumped out. As my grandmother told it, they had not gone more than a few feet when her father said, "Whoa. . . . Wait. . . . We haven't thanked you!" But to their amazement and wonder, they saw no one. The stranger had simply vanished into the night air!

The land was flat—no trees or obstructions—so the family could see for a great distance under the full moon and the now very clear night. It was a mystery, and they talked about it for many years afterwards.

Lucill M. Johnston

Lost and Found

I could not believe it! Here I was, forty-three years old and shopping with my mum, just like when I was five. Just as when I was young, Mum had gotten lost again and was wandering around the store, forgetting that I was with her as she became engrossed in aisle after aisle of fascinating merchandise. I looked up and down the aisles, but she was nowhere to be seen. Our golden rule for when we get separated still held, so I dutifully went to where I had last seen her and waited for her to find me.

The location was near the top of the escalator. What a great place to wait and people-watch! Total strangers walk into your view for a brief moment, then magically are carried away, never to be seen again.

Walking slowly, absentmindedly, toward me was a very elderly lady. It was Sunday and she was dressed for all the Sundays of her life. A delicate, tiny woman, she stood out among the crowd. Her pretty floral-print dress, coordinating jewelry, polished shoes, and white gloves showed a person who cared for herself.

With her head bowed over and her shoulders bent forward, her body language led me to wonder, *I am just half her age. What has this woman seen in her eighty-plus years? Death of loved ones, and a new awareness that her mornings of life are shortened?* Yet, here she was, dressed to face the world.

I thought of how people must feel as they age. It's as if they become invisible, as friends and family die. You go out and no one says, "Hi! How are you?" No one tells you how nice you look, or asks if that is a new dress. No one is left who really cares and has memories of you. When your close friends die, you must fade a little with each passing.

The tiny woman's eyes were focused on the floor in front of her, her expression saying that her mind was on another place or memory. She did not see the other shoppers as they passed. As the dainty woman approached, I said, "You look lovely in that dress. It really caught my eye."

For a brief moment her eyes sprang from her memory and focused on me, yet she still had that faraway gaze. She stepped carefully onto the escalator and started to glide away. Suddenly, she came to life. Her shoulders straightened and her eyes sparkled as she turned around and said, "Thank you, thank you! You have made my day!"

And the escalator carried her away forever, leaving me a changed person. For whatever my words meant to her, her gift of a smile will remain with me always. I no longer felt lost.

Mary Ellen Angelscribe

In the Midst of a Miracle

I am forty-three years old. When I was sixteen, my girl-friend, Sandy, became pregnant and gave our baby up for adoption. When I was nineteen, I married Sandy, and over the years we had three more children. Needless to say, for the last twenty-six years my wife has mourned the child she gave up. The baby was born on Valentine's Day 1971, and every Valentine's Day since has been a day of mourning in our household.

We had initiated a few searches for the child after she would have turned eighteen, but to no avail. We were listed in various agencies as looking and available for contact if our daughter initiated a search, but nothing came of this. Finally, my wife contacted an agency which was only paid if contact was made, so we were even more hopeful.

Shortly after this, I received my first contact from Mary Ellen. She was inquiring about my Internet screen name (DJU111). I told her I didn't know why, but 111 was always important to me. Mary Ellen replied that

111 indicated a connection with Angels and messengers. I didn't think too much about it and went on with my life.

On Friday, February 21, 1997, the search agency contacted my wife and informed her that they had information concerning our daughter. We were ecstatic. We sent the money overnight express to the searcher. On Saturday, we were expecting a phone call from them after they received the money.

Saturday morning was *hell.* Waiting for the call to arrive was so stressful. The call we had prayed for . . . waited for . . . for twenty-six years. At 11:00 A.M., I looked at the clock and thought, "The call will come in at 11:11," but did not say anything to my wife. I figured the moment was too tense already.

At exactly 11:11 A.M. the phone rang. It was the agency with the information. Now I knew we were in the realm of Angels, but I still didn't want to sound too corny. This is where it starts to get really weird.

We did find our daughter. She lives at 1111 Park Avenue. When my wife got pregnant, she lived at 111 Fourth Street. When we finally got up the nerve to make a call to my daughter, I looked at the clock and it was 1:11 P.M.

The miracle continued. Our newfound daughter promised to mail us photos of herself growing up. On Good Friday, I was off work and the mail came. We received the package that my wife and I were expecting but never really thought we would get. All I knew was, in it were pictures of the child we had given up for adoption twenty-six years before.

My wife did not have the day off, and I promised her that if the pictures came, I would bring them to her at work, so that together we could see our baby for the first time in twenty-six years.

I normally drive with the radio blasting. But on this day, my head was reeling and my nerves were shot, so I did not play the radio at all. I don't really know what was going through my mind as I drove. My mind was blank. I came to a red light and was in a trance. I just sat at the light with a blank stare.

At the intersection, there was a new car dealership, and although I was totally oblivious to the sounds around me, piercing through my trance came the sound of the receptionist at the car dealership paging over the car lot's intercom system, "John one eleven, John one eleven please." I immediately looked at my car clock and it was only a little after noon, or I would have surely flipped out. This was still quite surreal: There were those 1s again.

My wife works in the area where we grew up, so when she came out from work, I drove to the spot where I had asked her to marry me, when I was only fifteen years old. There in the parking lot of John the Baptist Church, she opened the package.

Our mental image of our oldest daughter now disappeared. In this package were actual pictures of her through the years. All of her birthdays, Christmases, First Communion in her white dress, teenage years, graduation—two decades of events, of a life we had not shared with her.

My first reaction surprised me, for it was of overwhelming gratitude to the people who raised her (a picture of them was also enclosed). These strangers gave my daughter a life I couldn't. And her life had been happy and good. Of course there was also an overwhelming feeling of loss, of what we missed.

When I got home, I tore the place apart looking for a copy of our Bible. I am not a religious person, so I wasn't sure where our Bible was, but I was very sure we had one. I went online looking for help to look up a passage from the Bible and then found the Bible at the same time. It was right next to the computer.

And John 1:11? "He came unto his own, and his own received him not." As I read these words, I realized that is exactly what happened to our daughter. She was born to us, her own, and we had received her not.

I know we are in the midst of something amazing, in more ways than one. I also have a deep feeling that it is not over yet. We intend to keep communication open with our daughter and see what develops. Obviously, we are taking it slowly. We do not want to do anything to mess it up. But I know I have been blessed.

David J. Uhrik, Sr.

Acknowledgments

I WOULD LIKE to acknowledge the following people who live their lives as Earth Angels and are great examples to all of us:

Anne Woods, my grandmother, who taught, through her living example, that the written word can effect positive changes in the world to help others.

Ellen Holden, my kind and loving mother, who teaches others to wear a smile even in adversity. Everyone should have a mother who smiles and can help with your spelling as you go through life.

Howard, my husband, who has a last name. Howard's support allows me to fly free and do what I need to do. He knows that when I have an idea in my head, the world will soon know of it. Howard, you are a brave man. Thanks for your patience and for listening to my wild and crazy dreams.

Ariel, my exceptionally gifted daughter. I admire your spirit, kindness, and the love you show toward others. I honor your many gifts and look forward to watching you bloom into the great woman you are destined to be.

Atira Hatton, my best friend and supporter. My sister not by birth but by choice. I admire your mystical gifts, which you share so lovingly with others. Thank you for trusting in me and the work I do, and supporting it with so much passion. P.S.—Thanks to your Master Guide from my Angels and me.

Mercia Kent, and Margaret and Walter Garry, family by choice.

Syd Simard, who when I was ill, taught me that one does not need a degree or training, but only love in one's heart, to heal another.

Dr. Robert Stillwell, one of the highest Earth Angels with whom I have ever had the privilege to walk in life. He lives and breathes spirituality and kindness each waking moment. It is an honor to call him friend.

Steve Koda, who gives his professional skills and support as gifts, and teaches others through his dedication to humankind.

Gary Hardin, for his support in believing in my angelic work. He was the first Angel author I met, and knowing him has led me on a wild journey.

Lori Jean Flory, who exudes love with every breath she takes, and who talks to Angels all the time.

John Harricharan, who walks the path of life with his guides as they teach unconditional love.

Marianne Williamson, Doreen Virtue, Ph. D., James Redfield, Neale D. Walsch, James Twyman, and Nick Bunick. Thank you for opening doors through which the world can come together in prayer to help heal the world. And for your belief in Angels.

Shirley MacLaine, for her brave spirit. She taught us that our heart and soul yearnings are normal.

A special note of thanks and a telepathic hug to all the folks who have contributed to this book and have touched our lives with their miracle stories. This book would not have been possible without you sharing your lives and stories with the world. Blessings and love to you all.

Thank you also to the *"Angels and Miracles"* prayer-team leader Judy Newman-Podlesny and the volunteers. These people of all beliefs, all ages, and from many different countries come together for the betterment and divine support of those in need. Can you imagine a group that is at the forefront of world peace? These are its members. This is the beginning.

Thanks also to Michael Baumann and Veronica Hamling, the brave souls who volunteered to create the Web page, and Angel artist Shirley Ann Morales. Meeting you all was by divine guidance and a miracle in action.

Blessings to Ines Flores, Naji Carera, Betty van Tulden, Rebecca Appehl and Joumana Medlej for volunteering their skills to translate the newsletter, thus inspiring others around the world.

Thanks to Dannion Brinkley, the C.I.A. Angel, who teaches Compassion In Action promoting hospice work.

And thanks to all the wonderful folks on the *Angels and Miracles Good-News-Letter* list, who have read and enjoyed the warm fuzzy e-mail. Thank you for sharing the stories with your friends, families, and loved ones. Because of each of you, the stories of love have circled the globe. It has been a joy to hear of your actions as Earth Angels in your own lives.

List of Contributors

Mary Ellen Angelscribe

Lou Ann Apostolopoulos

Dierdre Baker

Lin Bartlett

Kathy Berken

Lydia Brown

Nicole Burnham

Fran Churchill

Sue Covington

Matthew Dickerson

Carl Dixon

Helen Doyle

Julie Elmore

Jo Farrell

Bobbie Feinholz

John Fitch

Ardith Fowler

Carol Goldberg

Rich Greffrath

Jessica Hartig

Sally Harrington

Bonnie Hartin

Atira Hatton

Donna Hill

Laina Hill

Joy Howser

Maureen Johnson

Linda Johnston

Lucill M. Johnston

Veronica Kelly

Kathe Kenny

Lelander

Carletta Leonard
Kim Lively
Ursula J. Lovato
M'IxChel
Aynnie McAvoy
Sharon Mendenhall
Joanne Miller
Gail Mills
Scott Miners
Maria Morales
Grace Newman
Judy Newman
Robert E. Parrish, Ph.D.
Mary Beth Phillips
Jean Maurie Puhlman

Rikki Renshaw
Jamie Risinger
Eddie deRoulet
Kirk Schlea
Gayle Sieg
Myrna L. Smith
Marsha Stevens
Robert Stillwell, D.C.
Mary Ellen Szwejkowski
Ginger Talasco
Tania Teh Tanyong
Margaret S. Taylor
David J. Uhrik, Sr.
Doreen Virtue Ph.D.
Linda Watermeyer

Do You Have a Miracle to Share?

OVER THIRTY YEARS ago, when I was in high school, I read a true story that became the foundation of my spiritual beliefs. The story took place during World War I; a particular soldier just knew that "his side" was going to win the war because God was on his side.

Times were very hard for the fighting men. They did not have proper supplies, and they were cold and wet. One day the soldier came across the body of a dead "enemy" soldier. For a brief moment, as he focused on the dead man, he realized that the dead soldier was someone's son or father.

This only stopped him for a moment before he searched the man's body for something to add to his own physical comfort. What he found shocked him. Around the neck of the "enemy" was a medallion that said, "In God We Trust," in the language of the soldier's country.

This changed that man's life forever . . . and this story, my life. This man's experience let me see deeper into the hearts of all men and women. I was released from thinking that any one religion was the "only way" to touch the hand of God. I learned that all people seek to know God. Religions are the stepping stones of countries and cultures that individuals can take to understand the pull of their souls toward all that is divine.

It was a freeing experience to know that God places no restrictions on us, as other men's words had lead many of us to believe. It was then that I knew God would make the correct way known to each of us as we walked our life's paths.

I also learned that one person's story can change another person's life.

If you have a personal story that will open the hearts of others and touch them in miraculous ways, please share your experience with me. I would appreciate your help in teaching the world to EXPECT MIRACLES in their lives.

Please write to me:

Mary Ellen Angelscribe
P.O. Box 1074
Gig Harbor, Washington 98335

http://www.angelscribe.com

About the Author

Paula Iannuzzo

The creator of the Internet *Angels and Miracles Good-News-Letter,* Mary Ellen Angelscribe is a Canadian living in Washington with her daughter Ariel, husband Howard, pound pets, and, of course, her Angels.

CONARI PRESS, established in 1987, publishes books on topics ranging from psychology, spirituality, and women's history to sexuality, parenting, and personal growth. Our main goal is to publish quality books that will make a difference in people's lives—both how we feel about ourselves and how we relate to one another.

Our readers are our most important resource, and we value your input, suggestions, and ideas. We'd love to hear from you—after all, we are publishing books for you!

To request our latest book catalog, or to be added to our mailing list, please contact:

CONARI PRESS

2550 Ninth Street, Suite 101
Berkeley, California 94710-2551
800 685-9595   510-649-7175
fax: 510-649-7190   e-mail: conari@conari.com
http://www.readersNdex.com/conari/